Clean-Eating

BREAKFASTS
AND LUNCHES
MADE SIMPLE

**75 FLAVORFUL AND NUTRITIOUS RECIPES
THAT DITCH PROCESSED INGREDIENTS**

LACEY BAIER

CREATOR OF A SWEET PEA CHEF

PAGE STREET
PUBLISHING CO.

PAGE STREET
PUBLISHING CO.

First published in 2019 by
Page Street Publishing Co.
27 Congress Street, Suite 105
Salem, MA 01970
www.pagestreetpublishing.com

Distributed by Macmillan, sales in Canada by The Canadian Manda Group.

23 22 21 20 19   1 2 3 4 5

ISBN-13: 978-1-62414-840-8
ISBN-10: 1-62414-840-9

Library of Congress Control Number: 2019932080

Cover and book design by Rosie Stewart for Page Street Publishing Co.
Photography by Lacey Baier

Printed and bound in the United States

Dedication

TO MY LOBSTER

Contents

INTRODUCTION

Hey there, Lacey here!

I'm the writer and editor of A Sweet Pea Chef, a blog where I share easy, clean-eating recipes anyone can make. I'm so glad you're here. Let me start by asking you a question: Have you ever struggled with enjoying "healthy" food? Like enjoying it enough to stick with actually eating it?

I know I have!

My relationship with food has been a complicated one for as long as I can remember. I have always loved food a lot (duh—food's amazing, right?). The trouble was that it became obvious that I did. That's because I wasn't too fond of "healthy" foods . . . or moderation, really. Instead, I preferred comfort foods like pizza, burgers, tacos, pasta, and desserts. I still do, to be honest. But, after years of counting calories, trying various diets, losing weight, and gaining it right back again, I realized something had to change. For real. Not just for a limited period of time, but for good. That's when I decided to change my lifestyle and to embrace clean eating.

At the beginning, I was scared. The thought of never being able to enjoy a pizza or a slice of cheesecake terrified me, and made me nervous to even start. Would I enjoy a life without these foods I love, even if I was "healthier"? I wasn't sure. While I knew exactly how to end my struggle with weight, I was worried at what cost. I also knew I would miss my favorite foods and be unhappy. Who wants to eat bland chicken breast and raw carrot sticks for the rest of their life, y'know? Or never enjoy a birthday the same way because . . . no birthday cake is allowed. Not me!

After experimenting with a ton of different diets and fads, I realized I didn't have to give up my favorite foods. With clean eating and choosing whole, unrefined ingredients, I could eat nutritious meals without hating my food. That meant I didn't have to give up my favorite foods—all I had to do was adjust them a little bit. And this is true for you, too. Trust me, these clean-eating recipes will taste just as amazing as your favorite foods, but they will be good for your body, too! It's flipping awesome!

I'm seriously so glad my plan worked! Sometimes, I feel like I cheated because it's so simple. I manage to eat healthy, have fun, feel satisfied (this one's a biggie!), and create delicious recipes all at the same time.

Step by step, you can replace the processed, traditional ingredients you use with unprocessed, clean ones. It's not difficult, and I'm here to show you the way. It's actually very easy once you get the hang of it.

Why breakfasts and lunches for this cookbook? The answer is simple: because they're hard! Breakfasts and lunches are the meals that get rushed or even forgotten during the week, even though they have such an impact on our energy levels and mood during the day—not to mention our waistlines. Often they wind up being too boring, bland, or repetitive because people think there are only a few "healthy" options to make.

After reading this cookbook, I hope you'll be surprised by how many amazing options you actually have. Despite what you might think, clean-eating options for breakfast and lunch are by no means limited or boring—at least, they don't have to be. Even cooler—they don't have to be expensive, time-consuming, or super complicated either! Once you learn the basics and you start to get creative in the kitchen, the opportunities are endless.

Eating clean is about having control over the ingredients you put in your body. It's not a diet or a fad. It's a lifestyle—a clean and happy lifestyle that won't make you second guess if it's worth it. In fact, you'll love your food more than ever, because it's not only tasty, it will give you energy, help you maintain a healthy weight, and nourish your body. It's an opportunity to treat your body and mind as it deserves to be treated and to move beyond artificial, fake, and manufactured foods. Happy body, happy mind, happy life.

You'll learn that clean eating doesn't restrict calories or food groups. It's about balance, choosing the best foods from every food group, and combining them into well-balanced meals you'll love. Get ready to feel nourished and satisfied—something most "diets" definitely don't allow, and definitely something that was a big turnoff for me when I was desperately trying so many restrictive diets to lose weight.

I'm glad I have you on board, and I hope you're ready and excited to change your life for the better and to become a healthy, happy person who is able to enjoy favorite foods without stress. As you get started, make small changes and you will notice big differences. You don't have to give up processed ingredients all at once. Rather, reduce them one or two at a time. Then, once your body and tastes adjust, reduce additional unclean foods until eating clean becomes effortless. One day, you won't believe how much sugar and fake foods you were eating, and you'll get the simple pleasure of enjoying the natural sweetness of a carrot—I promise. This is an opportunity for you to take control of your food and your life.

Be mindful of what "clean living" really means—what's good and bad for you in foods and why it's so important to pay attention to those nutrition and ingredients labels on your food.

I know home cooking takes time and energy—something we're all short on. But preparing meals need not be a long or complicated process. Take advantage of the clean, delicious, and simple meals in this cookbook, many of which can be made ahead to save time during the week. Throughout this book, you'll see tips for which recipes can be made ahead easily and then stored in your fridge for up to 4 or 5 days, making them great grab-and-go meals. Even starting with one home-cooked breakfast or lunch in a week is a drastic improvement over eating at restaurants or choosing prepackaged foods.

I wish you the best of luck on your clean-eating journey, and I can't wait for you to discover how much you love your new clean lifestyle!

Let's get started!

THE 8 GUIDELINES TO CLEAN EATING

While eating clean is healthy, it's not quite the same as "healthy" eating. To make clean eating easier for you to understand and approach, I have identified eight basic guidelines to clean eating that will help you understand each food you choose. Now, there are always exceptions and allowances: that's why this is a list of guidelines, not a list of rules. Remember, I am here to make your life easier, not to restrict your options. Consider these tips for how to approach your clean-eating lifestyle.

1. COOK YOUR OWN FOOD

Cooking your own food gives you full control over the ingredients you're using to make your meals. You are able to skip ingredients or replace them with healthier options, which is not possible if you dine out, get takeout, or purchase prepared foods or mixes from the supermarket.

2. READ NUTRITION LABELS

You might be surprised how many seemingly simple ingredients are actually highly processed. Avoid anything that has words ending in "-ose," such as dextrose or fructose, on the nutritional label, because they might indicate added sugars, and avoid ingredients labeled as "modified" or "hydrolyzed," since those indicate the food is no longer in its natural, whole state and has been combined with manufactured, unhealthy chemicals or ingredients. Stay away from ingredients that are high in sodium or saturated fats, as the federal Food and Drug Administration recommends that we reduce these amounts as much as possible. The FDA advises that we limit sodium to no more than 20 percent of our daily calorie intake and saturated fat to no more than 20 grams, for someone on a 2,000-calorie daily diet.

3. EAT WHOLE FOODS

Processed or refined foods can contain added sugars, fats, and salt, but also preservatives and dyes. Skip the junk and opt for whole foods—whole grains, fresh fruits, fresh veggies, unsalted seeds and nuts, lean meats, dried beans or legumes, and full-fat dairy products.

4. AVOID PROCESSED FOODS

Besides more obviously processed foods, such as candy, chips, sugary sodas, and artificially flavored foods, there are other ones that are not as obvious, including fruit snacks, instant foods, energy bars, artificial sweeteners, and so on.

5. EAT WELL-BALANCED MEALS

Clean eating is not restrictive—it involves eating your favorite foods that are made with whole, unprocessed ingredients. Our bodies need all food groups incorporated into our diet, including protein, carbohydrates (or carbs), and fats.

6. LIMIT ADDED FAT, SALT, AND SUGAR

While it's not possible to remove these ingredients entirely from your diet, you can always limit them or opt for the healthiest form, such as eating fresh fruits or homemade clean desserts instead of desserts made with refined ingredients.

7. EAT 5 TO 6 MEALS PER DAY

Counting calories may seem important, but it prevents people from focusing on the nutritional benefits of the foods they are eating. Eating five to six meals per day—three main meals and two snacks—will prevent overeating, skipping meals, and feeling hungry. Believe it or not, if you're eating clean, you can feel full and satisfied and still lose weight, if that's your goal.

8. DON'T DRINK YOUR CALORIES

The more water you drink, the more you'll find you no longer want to drink soda or other drinks that are not nutritious or good for you. If you need some help increasing your water intake, try adding some fresh lemon juice or mint to your water.

EAT THIS, NOT THAT: INGREDIENT REPLACEMENT GUIDE

Before we jump into the recipes, here's a helpful list as you get started. You can refer to this replacement guide as an easy reference for what is refined versus unrefined. Switching to a clean lifestyle might seem complicated and hard . . . at least, it may at the beginning.

This replacement guide is to help make everything simple and easy for you. It's only complicated to choose the "right" ingredients when you don't know which ingredients are clean and which ones aren't. Long story short: eat real food. That means pay attention to what's in your food and, when possible, choose clean, whole, unprocessed ingredients.

Avoid This

REFINED SUGARS
Refined white sugar
Brown sugar
Artificial sweeteners

REFINED FLOUR
Refined/enriched flour
All-purpose flour
White flour

SATURATED FATS
Margarine
Bottled salad dressing
Canola oil
Soybean oil
Shortening

EMPTY CARBS
Store-bought granola
Candy and milk chocolate
Sugary soda

Fruit juices
Store-bought cereal
White breads
Pre-packaged pastries, cookies, and cakes
Chips
Ice cream

FATTY, HIGH-SODIUM PROTEINS
Bacon
Chicken skin
Processed deli meats
Fried/breaded foods
Hot dogs

REFINED THICKENERS
Cornstarch
All-purpose flour

Try This Instead

UNREFINED SUGARS
Pure maple syrup
Raw honey
Coconut sugar

CLEAN FLOURS
Whole wheat flour
Chickpea flour (gluten free, or GF)
Almond flour (GF)
Coconut flour (GF)
Quinoa flour (GF)
Spelt flour
Buckwheat flour (GF)

HEALTHY FATS
Unsalted, raw nuts
Coconut oil
Almond butter
Olive oil
Organic grass-fed butter
Natural peanut butter
Avocado
Avocado oil
Ghee
Seeds

GOOD, COMPLEX CARBS
Steel-cut oats
Rolled oats
Raw fruits, with skin when the skin is edible (e.g., apples, pears)
Whole grains

Vegetables
Brown rice
Sweet potatoes
Homemade clean desserts
Homemade clean cereal
Homemade clean baked goods
Dark chocolate
Soba noodles

LEAN PROTEIN
Eggs
Boneless, skinless chicken breast and thighs
Fish and seafood
Sugar- and nitrate-free bacon
Lean, organic grass-fed beef
Turkey breast
Chia seeds
Quinoa
Full-fat cottage cheese
Plain full-fat Greek yogurt

THICKENERS
Arrowroot starch
Tapioca starch
Potato starch
Chickpea flour

Satisfying
BREAKFAST BOWLS

Bursting with color and filled with clean and good-for-you ingredients, breakfast bowls are a very popular breakfast option in the healthy-eating community. While classic breakfasts can easily be made healthy, there is something very special about a breakfast bowl. Maybe it's the colors, the superfoods that get included, the delicious taste—or a combination of all these wonderful things. One thing is for sure—breakfast bowls rock. Not to mention, they look like a work of art, and they inspire you to be creative with your food, while maintaining your healthy lifestyle.

The thing I love the most about breakfast bowls is how versatile they are. You can make them sweet or savory, hot or cold. You can adjust them based on your mood. Or season. Or appetite. Or what you happen to have on hand. The possibilities are endless. Plus, I love the toppings!

To make a delicious and clean breakfast bowl, you mix a variety of ingredients, including whole grains, protein (such as Greek yogurt, eggs, or nuts), fruits, veggies, and other nutritious ingredients.

Breakfast bowls can build on the flavors of your favorite foods and desserts and still be an appropriate breakfast food. It's amazing and so fun to get creative! From replicating the familiar and yummy flavors of a blueberry muffin (page 14) or a carrot cake (page 18) in a sweet breakfast bowl to the savory and exciting flavors of huevos rancheros (page 22) or a breakfast burger (page 17), your morning meals are going to have so much flavor and life!

The bright, colorful, and fun breakfast bowls start here! You'll know how to make them, and which ingredients to combine to create a nutritionally balanced breakfast that looks appealing and is delicious to eat.

BLACKBERRY COBBLER GREEK YOGURT BOWL

This bowl has a blackberry cobbler granola that is mixed with yogurt and topped with fresh blackberries. The homemade blackberry granola, baked with fresh blackberries to give it that cobbler feeling, is super addictive, refined-sugar free, and made with oats, raw honey, vanilla extract, and cinnamon for extra flavor. And that's not even mentioning the pepitas, almonds, and coconut oil, all superfoods that are packed with fiber, protein, minerals, and vitamins. It's exactly what you'll expect from a sweet breakfast bowl—moderately sweet taste, color, texture, and lots of nutrients. Plus: Did you know you can make your own flavored yogurt at home and avoid the sugar and processed ingredients of store-bought yogurt?

FOR THE BLACKBERRY COBBLER GRANOLA

2 cups (200 g) rolled oats
½ cup (46 g) sliced raw almonds
½ cup (69 g) raw pepitas
3 tbsp (65 g) raw honey
2 tbsp (30 g) coconut oil, melted
½ tsp vanilla extract
½ tsp ground cinnamon
1½ cups (215 g) fresh blackberries, plus more for topping

FOR THE BOWLS

2 cups (480 g) plain full-fat Greek yogurt
2 tbsp (40 g) raw honey, plus more for topping
½ tsp vanilla extract

Preheat the oven to 350°F (180°C), and line a rimmed baking sheet with parchment paper.

To make the granola, in a large mixing bowl, combine the oats, almonds, pepitas, honey, coconut oil, vanilla, and cinnamon, and toss to coat. Carefully stir in the blackberries. Transfer the granola to the baking sheet and spread it out evenly.

Bake for 25 to 30 minutes, stirring one or two times. The granola is done when the oats smell toasted and are golden brown. Allow the granola to cool completely—it will harden as it cools.

For the bowls, mix the yogurt, honey, and vanilla in a large mixing bowl until it is combined well.

To serve, divide the flavored yogurt mixture between two bowls, and then top with the blackberry cobbler granola, fresh blackberries, and honey, if desired.

 Note: You can prepare the bowl and refrigerate it for up to 4 days in an airtight container. Top the yogurt with the granola when you are ready to eat the bowl, to keep the cobbler from getting soggy.

BLUEBERRY MUFFIN PORRIDGE BREAKFAST BOWL

Whole grains, such as oats, provide your body with lots of nutrients that are beneficial for your health. Eating whole grains is associated with lower blood pressure, a well-functioning digestive system, lower cholesterol, and a reduced risk of heart disease. This is why porridge is such a popular nutritious breakfast option. Porridge is amazing. If you have a sweet tooth, you can add pure maple syrup and enjoy it, guilt-free. Plus—it's very quick and easy to make and can be paired with so many other ingredients, including fruits and nuts.

For this bowl, I decided to combine porridge with the amazing flavors of blueberry muffins, because blueberry muffins are yummy, yes, but not always good for you. If you mix the flavors of blueberry muffins with porridge, you'll definitely get a clean-eating breakfast bowl. For extra fiber and protein, I add some chia seeds to the mix.

FOR THE PORRIDGE
1 cup (100 g) rolled oats
1 cup (240 ml) water
1 cup (240 ml) whole milk
1 cup (140 g) fresh blueberries, plus more for topping
2 tbsp (20 g) chia seeds
2 tbsp (30 ml) pure maple syrup, plus more for topping
¼ tsp ground cinnamon, plus more for topping
⅛ tsp sea salt
2 tsp (10 ml) vanilla extract

FOR SERVING
Chopped almonds, optional
Milk, optional
Plain full-fat Greek yogurt, optional

To make the porridge, place the oats, water, milk, blueberries, chia seeds, maple syrup, cinnamon, and salt in a medium saucepan. Stir to combine.

Cook over medium heat, stirring occasionally, until the mixture comes to a boil, about 5 minutes. Reduce the heat, and simmer until the oats have thickened and most of the berries have popped, making the porridge purple, about 5 more minutes. Remove the porridge from the heat, and stir in the vanilla.

For serving, transfer the porridge into two bowls, and top with blueberries, syrup, and cinnamon. Drizzle with the chopped almonds, a little milk, and a dollop of yogurt for additional texture, if desired.

BREAKFAST BURGER BOWL

What's the first thing that crosses your mind when you think about burgers? A family BBQ? A scrumptious dinner? A cheat day? Now, I want you to think about burgers for breakfast. Because, yes, burgers can be a breakfast option if you make a burger bowl. And, yes, they taste as amazing as they sound!

Personally, I love my burgers filled with fresh, whole ingredients, such as lean protein, fresh veggies, greens, and vibrant sauces. I like my Breakfast Burger Bowl the same way. I make the beef patties with organic grass-fed ground beef and pair them with hash browns, a maple-chipotle drizzle (that's heavenly!), and other tasty toppings, including sugar- and nitrate-free bacon, tomatoes, eggs, avocado, and arugula. Yum!

FOR THE MAPLE-CHIPOTLE DRIZZLE

½ cup (120 g) plain full-fat Greek yogurt

1 tbsp (15 ml) pure maple syrup

1 canned chipotle pepper in adobo sauce, minced

FOR THE PATTIES

½ lb (230 g) organic grass-fed ground beef

¼ tsp sea salt

⅛ tsp ground black pepper

⅛ tsp garlic powder

½ tbsp (8 ml) olive oil

FOR THE HASH BROWNS

2 medium russet potatoes, grated

¼ tsp sea salt

⅛ tsp ground black pepper

⅛ tsp garlic powder

FOR SERVING

2 slices sugar-free, nitrate-free bacon (I like Pederson's Uncured No Sugar Added Hickory Smoked)

1 tbsp (15 ml) olive oil

2 eggs

¼ tsp sea salt

⅛ tsp ground black pepper

1 cup (20 g) baby arugula

1 avocado, sliced

1 tomato, sliced

To make the maple-chipotle drizzle, combine the yogurt, maple syrup, and chipotle pepper in a small mixing bowl. Set it aside.

To make the patties, combine the beef, salt, pepper, and garlic powder in a large mixing bowl, and mix well. Shape into two even patties using your hands. Heat the olive oil over medium-high heat in a large skillet, and add the patties. Cook until the patties are cooked through and golden brown on both sides, 4 to 6 minutes per side. Remove the patties from the pan, and set them aside, covered loosely with aluminum foil to keep warm. Reserve the oil from the pan.

To make the hash browns, put the grated potatoes in the skillet used to cook the patties, and stir in the salt, pepper, and garlic powder. Cook until the potatoes are tender and golden, 8 to 10 minutes, tossing occasionally.

For serving, prepare the bacon and eggs while the potatoes are cooking. Fry the bacon, flipping occasionally, until crispy, 8 to 10 minutes, in a large skillet over medium-high heat. Drain the bacon on paper towels, and set it aside.

To fry the eggs, heat the olive oil in a skillet over medium-high heat until hot. Carefully add the eggs to the skillet, and season with the salt and pepper. To make the eggs sunny-side up, cover the pan with a lid for a minute or two, and don't flip the eggs. Once the egg whites are cooked, remove the eggs from the pan. For firmer yolks, flip the eggs when the whites are set (no longer jiggly), and cook them for an additional 1 to 2 minutes on the opposite side. Remove the eggs from the pan quickly to stop the cooking.

To serve, in each of two bowls, layer half of the hash browns, one burger patty, half of the arugula and avocado, the fried egg, and half of the tomato and bacon. Drizzle with the maple-chipotle topping.

CARROT CAKE QUINOA BOWLS

I'm not going to recommend a slice of sugar-filled cake, don't worry. But I will recommend a Carrot Cake Quinoa Bowl! These bowls are packed with superfoods and totally make you feel like you're eating a big, thick slice of carrot cake. Sounds amazing, right? Well, there's more! The bowl is drizzled with a sweet Greek yogurt sauce that brings all the breakfast bowl flavors together. Yes, please!

FOR THE GREEK YOGURT DRIZZLE

½ cup (120 g) plain full-fat Greek yogurt
¾ cup (180 ml) pure maple syrup
½ tsp vanilla extract
1–2 tbsp (15–30 ml) unsweetened coconut milk, divided

FOR THE BOWLS

1½ cups (255 g) quinoa
3 cups (720 ml) unsweetened coconut milk, plus more for serving, optional
1½ cups (165 g) grated carrots
2 tsp (5 g) ground cinnamon
½ tsp ground nutmeg
¼ tsp ground ginger
⅛ tsp sea salt
3 tbsp (45 ml) pure maple syrup, plus more for topping
1 tbsp (16 g) almond butter, plus more for topping
1 tsp vanilla extract

FOR SERVING

⅓ cup (36 g) chopped pecans
¼ cup (36 g) golden raisins

To prepare the Greek yogurt drizzle, stir together the yogurt, maple syrup, and vanilla. Add the coconut milk, 1 tablespoon (15 ml) at a time, if it's needed to make the mixture the consistency of icing. Refrigerate the drizzle while you prepare the quinoa.

To make the bowls, rinse the quinoa in a fine-mesh sieve to remove any debris and dirt. In a medium saucepan, cook the quinoa over medium-high heat for 6 to 8 minutes, tossing frequently, to toast. It's done when the quinoa is no longer wet and begins to pop and turn golden brown. Add the coconut milk to the saucepan, and reduce the heat to medium. Once the mixture starts to boil, add the carrots, cinnamon, nutmeg, ginger, and salt, and stir to combine. Lower the heat to a simmer. Cover the pan, and simmer the mixture until the liquid has been fully absorbed and the quinoa has doubled in size, 15 to 20 minutes. Fluff the quinoa with a fork.

Remove the quinoa from the heat. Stir in the maple syrup, almond butter, and vanilla, until everything is combined and smooth.

For serving, divide the quinoa into four bowls. Top each portion with extra coconut milk, if desired, maple syrup, almond butter, pecans, and raisins. Drizzle one-quarter of the Greek yogurt drizzle over each bowl.

 Note: The quinoa mixture can be made up to 5 days ahead and refrigerated in an airtight container. Reheat it in the microwave. Add the yogurt drizzle and toppings just before serving.

GREEN GODDESS BLUEBERRY YOGURT BOWL

Combining superfoods, like kale, spinach, blueberries, and avocado, in a breakfast bowl results in two very important things: (1) a super delicious breakfast bowl, and (2) your food being packed with proteins, fibers, good fats, and nutrients that will do wonders for your health. And it's so easy to do it, too. No magic involved. Just a few easy steps.

FOR THE BOWLS

2 cups (60 g) baby spinach
1 cup (240 g) plain full-fat Greek yogurt
Small handful of kale, stems removed
1 ripe banana
½ avocado
2 tbsp (32 g) almond butter
1 tsp matcha powder

FOR SERVING

1 cup (140 g) fresh blueberries
Raw pepitas, optional
Unsweetened shredded coconut, optional
Sliced kiwi, optional
Hemp seed hearts, optional

For the bowls, combine the spinach, yogurt, kale, banana, avocado, almond butter, and matcha powder in a food processor or high-speed blender. Blend until smooth and creamy, then divide between two bowls.

For serving, top the yogurt mixture with the blueberries, pepitas, coconut, kiwi, and hemp seed hearts, if desired.

Note: Superfoods are not ingredients that have magical powers. They are whole ingredients and very rich in important nutrients. Kale, for example, is seen as a superfood . . . for good reason. Kale contains many nutrients, including minerals—such as calcium, magnesium, and zinc—and vitamins—such as C, K, and B6. Kale is also high in fiber. Pretty much the same can be said about spinach. Avocado is a great source of healthy fats and potassium, and it's rich in vitamins—such as B5, B6, K, and E. Plus, it's super yummy.

HUEVOS RANCHEROS BREAKFAST BOWL

Huevos rancheros is a Mexican breakfast dish that's comforting, delicious, and super satisfying. To transform the classic into a clean breakfast bowl, I replaced the Mexican rice with potatoes, made a clean ranchero sauce from scratch (yum!), and paired everything with clean-eating refried black beans, fried eggs, and clean corn tortillas. It still sounds hearty and delicious, doesn't it? That's because it is. But it's also a healthy and balanced breakfast bowl. So easy, yet so *delicioso*.

FOR THE POTATOES

2 medium unpeeled russet potatoes, diced
1 tbsp (15 ml) olive oil
1 tsp sea salt
1 tsp paprika
½ tsp chili powder
¼ tsp garlic powder

FOR THE SAUCE

1 tbsp (15 ml) olive oil
½ medium yellow onion, diced
½ large red bell pepper, diced
½ large green bell pepper, diced
½ large poblano pepper, diced
½ jalapeño pepper, seeded and finely diced
2 cloves garlic, minced
½ tsp sea salt, plus more to taste
¼ tsp ground cumin
¼ tsp ground black pepper, plus more to taste
¼ tsp dried oregano
⅛ tsp cayenne pepper
1½ cups (270 g) diced tomatoes
½ cup (120 ml) low-sodium chicken broth
¼ cup (4 g) chopped fresh cilantro

FOR THE REFRIED BLACK BEANS

1 (15-oz [425-g]) can black beans with no salt added, drained and rinsed
1 tsp chili powder
½ tsp ground cumin
1 tbsp (15 ml) freshly squeezed lime juice
½ tsp sea salt

For the potatoes, preheat the oven to 400°F (200°C), and line a rimmed baking sheet with parchment paper. On the baking sheet, toss the potatoes, olive oil, salt, paprika, chili powder, and garlic powder to coat. Bake for 20 to 25 minutes, or until the potatoes are tender. Toss halfway through for even browning.

Prepare the sauce while the potatoes are in the oven. Heat the olive oil in a large skillet or saucepan over medium-high heat. Add the onion, red and green peppers, poblano pepper, jalapeño, and garlic. Cook, stirring occasionally, for 6 to 8 minutes, or until the onion begins to soften.

Add the salt, cumin, pepper, oregano, and cayenne, and stir to combine. Add the tomatoes and chicken broth, and bring the sauce to a simmer. Cover, and simmer for 15 minutes.

Remove the cover, stir in the cilantro, and cook for 5 to 8 minutes, or until the sauce begins to thicken. Season with salt and pepper, to taste.

Prepare the beans while the sauce is cooking. In a small pot, use a potato masher to mash together the beans, chili powder, cumin, lime juice, and salt. Cook over medium-high heat, mashing and stirring occasionally, for 7 to 8 minutes, or until heated through.

(CONTINUED)

FOR THE CORN TORTILLAS

2–4 tbsp (30–60 ml) olive oil, divided
4 corn tortillas

FOR THE EGGS

1 tbsp (15 ml) olive oil
4 eggs
½ tsp sea salt
¼ tsp ground black pepper

FOR SERVING

Chopped fresh cilantro
Queso fresco cheese, crumbled
Lime wedges

To prepare the corn tortillas, line a plate with paper towels. Heat ½ tablespoon (8 ml) of the olive oil in a large skillet. Add 1 tortilla to the oil, and cook for 1 to 2 minutes per side, flipping frequently, until both sides are beginning to bubble and turn golden. Remove the tortilla from the pan, and lay it on the prepared plate to drain. Repeat with the remaining tortillas, adding the remaining olive oil, ½ tablespoon (8 ml) at a time, as needed to keep the tortilla bubbling and frying.

To fry the eggs, heat the olive oil over medium-high heat in a skillet until hot. Carefully add the eggs to the skillet. Season with the salt and pepper. To make the eggs sunny-side up, cover the pan with a lid for a minute or two, and don't flip the eggs. Once the egg whites are cooked, remove the eggs from the pan and serve. For firmer yolks, flip the eggs when the whites are set (no longer jiggly), and cook them for an additional 1 to 2 minutes on the opposite side. Remove the eggs from the pan quickly to stop the cooking.

For serving, in each of four bowls, layer one-quarter of the refried beans, followed by one-quarter of the ranchero sauce, a tortilla, one-quarter of the potatoes, then a fried egg. Garnish with the cilantro, queso fresco, and a lime wedge.

 Note: This recipe is great for an advance meal-prep breakfast. The bowl will last in the fridge for up to 4 days, stored in an airtight container. To keep the tortillas as crispy as possible, store separately and then top when ready to serve.

SAVORY SWEET POTATO BOWL
with SALSA VERDE

This bowl contains everything a breakfast should: fiber, protein, whole grains, and superfoods. To make it good for you, I pair roasted sweet potatoes with quinoa, sautéed kale, a 10-minute homemade salsa verde to die for, and a poached egg. Yum! This colorful savory breakfast bowl is for sure a great way to start your day filled with energy.

FOR THE SALSA VERDE

10 tomatillos, husked and quartered

1 jalapeño pepper, seeded and halved

2 cloves garlic, unpeeled

1 poblano chile, seeded and halved

⅓ cup (5 g) fresh cilantro, stems removed

Freshly squeezed juice of 1 lime

½ tsp sea salt

FOR THE ROASTED SWEET POTATOES AND ONIONS

2 large sweet potatoes, diced

1 large red onion, diced

1½ tbsp (22 ml) olive oil

½ tsp garlic powder

½ tsp curry powder

¼ tsp ground cumin

½ tsp sea salt

⅛ tsp ground black pepper

FOR THE QUINOA

1 cup (180 g) quinoa

2 cups (480 ml) water

½ tsp sea salt

¼ tsp garlic powder

FOR THE SAUTÉED KALE

1 tbsp (15 ml) olive oil

1 clove garlic, minced

4 cups (270 g) chopped kale

¼ tsp sea salt

⅛ tsp ground black pepper

To make the salsa verde, preheat the broiler to high, and line a baking sheet with aluminum foil or parchment paper. Place the tomatillos, jalapeño, garlic, and poblano on the baking sheet and broil for 5 to 10 minutes, or until everything is nicely charred.

Remove the peel from the garlic, then place the tomatillo mixture in a blender, along with the cilantro, lime juice, and salt. Blend until smooth, and then set aside.

For the potatoes, preheat the oven to 400°F (200°C), and line a baking sheet with parchment paper. On the baking sheet, toss the sweet potatoes, onion, olive oil, garlic powder, curry powder, cumin, salt, and pepper to coat. Roast for 25 to 30 minutes, until the sweet potatoes are tender when pierced with a knife.

Make the quinoa while the sweet potatoes are in the oven. Rinse the quinoa in a fine-mesh sieve to remove any debris and dirt. In a medium saucepan, cook the quinoa over medium-high heat for 6 to 8 minutes, tossing frequently, to toast the quinoa. It's done when the quinoa is no longer wet and begins to pop and turn golden brown. Add the water, salt, and garlic powder. Bring the water to a boil. Cover the pan, reduce the heat to low, and let the quinoa simmer, for 15 to 20 minutes, or until all the water has been absorbed and the quinoa is doubled in size. Fluff the quinoa with a fork, and set aside.

To sauté the kale, heat a large skillet over medium-high heat, and add the olive oil. When the olive oil is hot, add the garlic, and stir it for 1 minute, or until fragrant. Add the kale, salt, and pepper to the skillet, and cook for 5 to 7 minutes, or until the kale has reduced in size, wilted, and is tender. Toss the kale frequently.

(CONTINUED)

SAVORY SWEET POTATO BOWL
with SALSA VERDE (CONTINUED)

FOR THE POACHED EGGS
6 cups (1.4 L) water
1 tbsp (15 ml) rice vinegar
4 eggs

To poach the eggs, add enough of the water needed to fill a saucepan two-thirds full. Bring the water to a boil over high heat. Reduce the heat until you see bubbles on the surface; the water shouldn't be at a rolling boil. Stir the vinegar into the water.

Line a plate with a paper towel. Crack one egg into a small cup with a handle, carefully lower the cup into the water, then tip it to put the egg into the water. Cook the egg for 4 minutes to create a firm white and a soft and runny yolk. Using a slotted spoon, remove the egg from the water, and set it on the prepared plate to drain. Repeat with the remaining eggs.

In each of four bowls, arrange one-quarter each of the quinoa, roasted sweet potatoes, and sautéed kale. Top each with a poached egg, and then drizzle the bowls with the salsa verde.

 Note: Sweet potatoes are among the healthiest foods you can eat. They are filled with nutrients, including vitamins A, C, and B, and minerals, such as potassium, manganese, phosphorus, and copper. Sweet potatoes are also an amazing source of fiber and low in calories. Not to mention, they are super versatile, which means they can be turned into so many different dishes—both sweet and savory.

On the Griddle

LOW-CARB, HIGH-PROTEIN PANCAKES AND WAFFLES

If the world of clean-eating pancakes and waffles is new to you, this chapter will be your guide. There's just something about waffles and pancakes that is so comforting and filling—they seem like they're bad for us. However, by simply replacing a few refined ingredients with unrefined, more nutritious ones, you can make delicious and nutritious pancakes at home without a boxed mix!

If you're more into the sweet side, you'll love the Sweet Potato Chocolate Chip Pancakes (page 43), which are so rich, chocolaty, and naturally sweet, and the Protein Peaches-and-Cream Pancakes (page 40), which are a little lighter, but full of juicy peach flavor and sweet cream. If you like more savory flavors, say hello to the coolest Low-Carb Pizza Waffles (page 39) ever, made with cauliflower in the crust and packed full of pizza flavors. You're not gonna believe you're eating unrefined, whole foods that will nourish your body!

(NOT SO) CHUNKY MONKEY WAFFLES

Chunky monkey waffles are like the ultimate sweet treat and breakfast combined. We're talking about banana, chocolate, and nuts paired with the amazing fluffiness of waffles. Instead of being loaded with carbs, refined sugar, and fats, these waffles are packed with protein, fiber, and nutrients. How did I make that possible? I replace all-purpose flour with rolled oats, I skip sugar and use a ripe banana, I replace the chocolate chunks with chocolate protein powder, and I add a little bit of natural peanut butter for extra protein and taste. Doesn't sound hard, am I right?

But to get that chunky monkey style, you need toppings. I make a rich chocolate sauce with Greek yogurt for these waffles, because that is a must for chunky monkey anything. Dark chocolate chips, banana slices, and chopped peanuts make my (Not So) Chunky Monkey Waffles complete.

FOR THE CHOCOLATE SAUCE
2 tbsp (30 g) plain full-fat Greek yogurt
1 tbsp (15 ml) pure maple syrup
1 tbsp (5 g) unsweetened cocoa powder
1 tbsp (15 ml) unsweetened almond milk

FOR THE WAFFLES
⅓ cup (30 g) rolled oats
¼ cup (19 g) chocolate protein powder (I like Naked Nutrition)
2 tbsp (32 g) natural peanut butter
1 ripe banana, mashed
2 egg whites
½ tsp baking powder
¼ tsp cinnamon
½ tsp vanilla extract
1 tbsp (15 ml) unsweetened almond milk
Coconut oil, for greasing the waffle iron

FOR SERVING
Chopped peanuts
1 ripe banana, sliced
Dark chocolate chips

To make the chocolate sauce, in a small bowl, whisk together the yogurt, maple syrup, cocoa powder, and almond milk until smooth. Set aside.

To make the waffles, in a food processor or blender, combine the oats, protein powder, peanut butter, banana, egg whites, baking powder, cinnamon, vanilla, and almond milk. Blend until smooth.

Heat a waffle iron, and grease it with coconut oil. Spoon about ¼ cup (60 ml) of the batter onto the hot iron, and cook the waffle for 3 to 4 minutes, or until golden brown. Repeat with the remaining batter. Cover the cooked waffles with a clean kitchen towel to keep them warm. (You can also keep them warm, on a baking sheet lined with parchment paper, in a preheated 200°F [93°C] oven.)

For serving, top the waffles with the chocolate sauce, peanuts, banana, and chocolate chips.

CHILE-CHOCOLATE WAFFLES

Chile-Chocolate Waffles are such a delight. If you've never tried chili powder in waffles, don't worry, it won't make the waffles super spicy. It will just give them that extra touch that makes food go from good to *amazing*.

The best part of these spicy chocolate waffles is the combination of flavors. You have the rich, sweet chocolate with the kick of heat paired with a little sweet pure maple syrup, tart, cool fresh berries, and a scoop of plain full-fat Greek yogurt for a creamy component healthier than whipped cream. That's it! You've got yourself a rich, decadent-looking breakfast that tastes incredible and is not that decadent, after all.

FOR THE WAFFLES
1 cup (96 g) whole wheat pastry flour
¼ cup (20 g) unsweetened cocoa powder
2 tbsp (20 g) coconut sugar
2 tsp (8 g) baking powder
1 tsp chili powder, plus more for garnish
1 tsp ground cinnamon
¼ tsp sea salt
1 cup (240 ml) unsweetened almond milk
1 egg
2 tbsp (30 g) coconut oil, melted, plus more for greasing the waffle iron
1 tsp vanilla extract

FOR SERVING
Fresh berries
Pure maple syrup
Plain full-fat Greek yogurt

To make the waffles, place the flour, cocoa powder, coconut sugar, baking powder, chili powder, cinnamon, and salt in a large bowl. Whisk together to combine.

In a separate bowl, whisk together the milk, egg, coconut oil, and vanilla. Pour the milk mixture into the flour mixture, and then whisk together until a smooth batter is formed. Do not overmix.

Preheat the waffle iron, and grease it with the coconut oil. Pour ⅓ cup (80 ml) of the batter onto the hot waffle iron and close it.

Cook until the waffles are crisp and cooked through, 4 to 6 minutes, depending on the size and shape of your waffle iron.

For serving, top the waffles with a light sprinkle of chili powder and the berries, maple syrup, and yogurt.

KEY LIME PROTEIN PANCAKES

If you've ever had a bite of key lime pie, you know the fresh taste, intense aroma, and the citrus flavor. Now you can enjoy the same burst of lime in these fluffy, amazing pancakes!

First off, there's no need to find key limes—any fresh limes will do the trick. The protein-packed formula for these pancakes includes vanilla protein powder, rolled oats, and almond flour. Pancakes are just not complete without toppings. So, to add even more lime deliciousness, I make a creamy lime topping with Greek yogurt, pure maple syrup, vanilla extract, and fresh lime zest. Yum!

Can you believe this finger-licking goodness is good for you? You better, because these Key Lime Protein Pancakes are nutritious and delicious.

FOR THE CREAMY LIME TOPPING
½ cup (120 g) plain full-fat Greek yogurt
1 tbsp (15 ml) pure maple syrup
⅛ tsp vanilla extract
¼ tsp lime zest

FOR THE PANCAKES
¾ cup (75 g) rolled oats
½ cup (60 g) almond flour
½ cup (38 g) vanilla protein powder (I like Naked Nutrition)
2 tsp (8 g) baking powder
1 tsp baking soda
¼ tsp sea salt
¼ cup (60 ml) freshly squeezed lime juice
¼ cup (60 ml) unsweetened almond milk
2 egg whites
2 tbsp (30 ml) pure maple syrup, plus more for topping
1 tsp lime zest, plus more for topping
Coconut oil, for greasing the pan

To make the creamy lime topping, combine the yogurt, maple syrup, vanilla, and lime zest in a small bowl, and stir until well mixed. Set aside.

For the pancakes, place the oats, almond flour, protein powder, baking powder, baking soda, and salt in a mixing bowl. Whisk to combine.

In a separate bowl, whisk together the lime juice, milk, egg whites, maple syrup, and lime zest.

Add the milk mixture to the oat mixture, and stir until just combined. Do not overmix.

Preheat a griddle or a skillet over medium heat and grease lightly with coconut oil.

Pour ¼ cup (60 ml) of the batter onto the griddle, and gently spread it into a circle shape, using the measuring cup or by tilting the griddle.

Cook until the edges start to become crisp and look dull, 2 to 3 minutes. Flip the pancake and cook for another 1 to 2 minutes. Repeat with the remaining batter.

To serve, top the pancakes with the creamy lime topping, a drizzle of maple syrup, and lime zest.

LEMON POPPY SEED PANCAKES

The poppy seeds in these pancakes are responsible for the crunchiness, the cottage cheese adds so much creamy softness and protein, and the lemon makes the flavor of the pancakes out-of-this-world good. For more goodness, I top these pancakes with a delicious homemade lemon yogurt topping and a few fresh blueberries.

FOR THE LEMON YOGURT TOPPING

¼ cup (60 g) plain full-fat Greek yogurt

1 tbsp (15 ml) pure maple syrup

1 tsp freshly squeezed lemon juice

¼ tsp lemon zest, plus more for topping

FOR THE LEMON POPPY SEED PANCAKES

¾ cup (160 g) full-fat cottage cheese

2 eggs

1 tbsp (6 g) lemon zest

¼ cup (60 ml) freshly squeezed lemon juice

2 tbsp (30 ml) pure maple syrup

1⅓ cups (130 g) rolled oats

1 tbsp (12 g) baking powder

⅛ tsp sea salt

2 tsp (6 g) poppy seeds

1–2 tbsp (15–30 ml) water, divided, optional

Coconut oil, for greasing the pan

½ cup (70 g) fresh blueberries

To make the lemon yogurt topping, combine the yogurt, maple syrup, lemon juice, and lemon zest in a small mixing bowl. Set it aside.

For the pancakes, combine the cottage cheese, eggs, lemon zest, lemon juice, maple syrup, oats, baking powder, salt, and poppy seeds in a blender. Blend until mixed well. If the batter is too thick, add 1 tablespoon (15 ml) of the water at a time, until the batter is a pourable, but not watery, consistency.

Heat a griddle or large skillet over medium heat, and grease it with the coconut oil. Once the pan is hot, spoon about ¼ cup (60 ml) of the batter into a 4-inch (10-cm) circle, and let the pancake cook 2 to 3 minutes until the edges look dull, a few small bubbles appear on the top in the center, and the underside is golden brown. Flip carefully, and continue to cook until the second side is golden brown, 2 to 3 minutes.

Remove the pancake from the heat, and repeat with the remaining batter, adding more coconut oil for greasing the griddle, if needed.

To serve, drizzle the yogurt sauce over the pancakes, and top them with the blueberries and lemon zest.

Note: These pancakes can be made ahead and refrigerated in an airtight container for up to 4 days until you are ready to enjoy them.

LOW-CARB PIZZA WAFFLES

Is it a stretch to say that pizza is everybody's favorite food? I also believe waffles are one of the most well-loved breakfast foods. One day, I was wondering . . . what would happen if I put these two together? Pizza waffles? What sounded like a crazy thought initially turned into a delicious meal that can be enjoyed for breakfast, lunch, and dinner. These waffles are life-changing.

To make pizza waffles, I combine cauliflower, the secret ingredient that makes these waffles low-carb, with whole wheat pastry flour, two types of cheese—mozzarella and Parmesan—dried herbs, uncured pepperoni, and the traditional waffle ingredients—milk, eggs, and baking powder. Because most of the pizza ingredients are incorporated in the waffles, the toppings have to stay fresh and simple. So, I opt for fresh parsley and a tomato sauce for dipping.

Who would've thought it's so easy to create the breakfast, lunch, or dinner of your dreams?

FOR THE WAFFLES

3 cups (255 g) riced cauliflower
(see Note)

1 cup (96 g) whole wheat pastry flour

½ cup (120 ml) unsweetened almond milk

½ cup (57 g) chopped fresh mozzarella cheese

15 slices uncured pepperoni, chopped

2 eggs

2 tbsp (10 g) grated Parmesan cheese

2 tsp (8 g) baking powder

½ tsp sea salt

½ tsp garlic powder

½ tsp onion powder

½ tsp dried oregano

½ tsp dried basil

¼ tsp ground black pepper

Olive oil, for greasing the waffle iron

FOR SERVING

Chopped fresh Italian parsley

½ cup (120 ml) marinara sauce with no added sugar

Chopped mozzarella

Grated Parmesan

Chopped pepperoni

To make the waffles, place the cauliflower, flour, milk, mozzarella, pepperoni, eggs, Parmesan, baking powder, salt, garlic powder, onion powder, oregano, basil, and pepper in a large mixing bowl. Mix until the ingredients are well combined.

Heat up your waffle iron, then grease it with the olive oil. Depending on the size of your waffle iron, pour one-quarter or one-half of the batter onto the surface. Make sure to cover the entire waffle area, as this mixture will not spread when it cooks, as other waffle batter does. My waffle iron is large and uses approximately 1 cup (240 ml) of the mixture.

Cook for 4 to 6 minutes, or until the waffle is golden brown on both sides and releases easily from the waffle iron. You'll notice the amount of steam reduces significantly from the waffle iron as the waffle nears being ready. Repeat until you've used all the remaining waffle mixture.

For serving, garnish the waffles with the parsley, marinara sauce, mozzarella, Parmesan, and pepperoni. Serve with a small bowl of the marinara sauce, for dipping.

 Note: Riced cauliflower is one of my favorite clean, low-carb substitutions. I make mine in a food processor, pulsing a head of roughly chopped cauliflower in short bursts until it reaches the consistency of rice. You can also use a kitchen grater, just as you would grate cheese, to rice cauliflower. A 1-pound (455-g) head of cauliflower yields about 4 cups of cauliflower rice. To save time, you can buy riced cauliflower at most grocery stores. It's usually in the frozen food section, but some stores sell cauliflower rice in the produce department.

PROTEIN PEACHES-*and*-CREAM PANCAKES

One of my favorite things is to use fresh, seasonal fruits and veggies in my recipes. These peach pancakes combine the natural sweetness of peaches with cinnamon and other spices that make the fruit taste better. The natural fruit syrup is just amazing over pancakes. Add a clean-eating cream to the mix, and the breakfast becomes a wonderful experience.

FOR THE CREAM
½ cup (120 g) plain full-fat Greek yogurt
1 tbsp (15 ml) pure maple syrup, plus more for topping
½ tsp vanilla extract

FOR THE PEACHES
2 large peaches, peeled and sliced
1½ tbsp (15 g) coconut sugar
¼ tsp ground cinnamon
2 tbsp (30 ml) water

FOR THE PANCAKES
1½ cups (144 g) whole wheat pastry flour
2 tbsp (14 g) ground flaxseed
2 tbsp (20 g) coconut sugar
1 tsp baking soda
1 tsp baking powder
⅛ tsp sea salt
1–1¼ cups (240–300 ml) unsweetened almond milk, divided
2 egg whites
1 tsp vanilla extract
Coconut oil, for greasing the pan

For the cream, combine the yogurt, maple syrup, and vanilla in a small bowl. Refrigerate the cream until you are ready to use it.

For the peaches, in a small saucepan, combine the peaches, coconut sugar, cinnamon, and water. Simmer gently over medium heat, stirring occasionally, until the peaches are soft, 6 to 8 minutes. Set the pan aside.

For the pancakes, combine the flour, flaxseed, coconut sugar, baking soda, baking powder, and salt in a large mixing bowl. Whisk together well.

In a separate mixing bowl, combine 1 cup (240 ml) of the almond milk, the egg whites, and vanilla, and mix well.

Pour the milk mixture into the flour mixture, and whisk them together. Add more of the remaining ¼ cup (60 ml) of milk, a little at a time, if it's needed to reach a thick, but pourable consistency. Let the batter stand for 5 minutes. It will thicken as it sets.

Heat a griddle or skillet over medium-high heat until hot. Lightly grease it with the coconut oil. Pour ¼ cup (60 ml) of the batter onto the griddle in a circle. Cook the pancake, 2 to 4 minutes, until bubbles form on the surface and the bottom is golden. Flip the pancake, and cook until done, about 1 more minute. Repeat with all of the remaining batter.

For serving, top the pancakes with the yogurt topping, and then the warm peaches.

Note: If you're unable to use fresh peaches, frozen peach slices will work great in this recipe.

SWEET POTATO CHOCOLATE CHIP PANCAKES

These pancakes are sweet, thick, rich, fluffy, and, of course, good for your body and taste buds. They use rolled oats instead of all-purpose flour to create totally unrefined, but still delicious, pancakes. To add extra deliciousness, stuff them with chocolate chips. The sweet potato–chocolate combination is one you never thought you needed in your life, but you most definitely do.

To serve the pancakes, go for classic and nutritious toppings. I like my Sweet Potato Chocolate Chip Pancakes with pure maple syrup and banana slices. OK, and maybe some more dark chocolate chips!

FOR THE PANCAKES

1 cup (255 g) cooked and mashed sweet potato
¾ cup (180 ml) unsweetened almond milk
⅔ cup (60 g) rolled oats
1 egg
½ tsp ground cinnamon
½ tsp vanilla extract
2 tsp (8 g) baking powder
⅛ tsp ground nutmeg
⅛ tsp sea salt
2 tbsp (20 g) dark chocolate chips, plus more for topping
1 tbsp (15 g) coconut oil, melted and divided

FOR SERVING

Pure maple syrup
1 ripe banana, sliced

To make the pancakes, place the sweet potato, milk, oats, egg, cinnamon, vanilla, baking powder, nutmeg, and salt in a blender or food processor. Blend until completely smooth. Fold in the chocolate chips.

Heat about 1 teaspoon of the coconut oil over medium-high heat in a griddle or skillet. Once the pan is hot, pour about ¼ cup (60 ml) of the batter onto the surface.

Cook the pancake for 3 to 4 minutes, until the edges begin to turn from shiny to dull and bubbles appear in the center of the pancake. The entire top of the pancake should look dull. The pancake will be tender, so flip carefully.

Flip and cook for an additional 2 to 3 minutes, or until golden brown. Repeat with the remaining batter, adding more of the remaining coconut oil, a teaspoon at a time, to grease the griddle, as needed.

For serving, top the pancakes with the chocolate chips, maple syrup, and banana slices.

Note: If you eat gluten-free, be sure to use gluten-free oats in these clean-eating recipes.

Beyond Basic Oatmeal

DELICIOUS PREP-AHEAD OVERNIGHT OATS

Oats are not only the healthiest whole grain and a very healthy breakfast option, but they are also one of the healthiest foods ever. And I'm talking about all types of foods here. Oats are that amazing, yes. In case you don't know why, it's because oats are a great source of fiber, vitamins, antioxidants, and minerals. They also contain protein and fats in larger amounts than other grains, which means they have tons of health benefits, including lower cholesterol and blood sugar, a reduced risk of heart disease, reduced inflammation, and improved digestive system health. Overall, we can say without a doubt that oats are an amazing way to start the day.

Oats are commonly eaten as oatmeal for breakfast. It's filling, it's good for you, it's energizing, and, on top of everything, it's easy to make. But cooking oats takes time, which is why most people, including me, prefer overnight oats, which are quick and easy to prep and just as versatile as regular oatmeal.

A quick and easy-to-make breakfast? Who doesn't want that? Especially since our mornings are too hectic to have time for a proper, well-balanced meal. Except . . . it's not hard at all to have a proper breakfast when it is made overnight, while you sleep, and with just a little prep. It's the best way to make sure that, no matter how busy and hectic mornings are, skipping breakfast is no longer an option, because you have tasty, clean-eating oats waiting for you in the fridge.

This chapter will show you how easy it is to make oats taste amazing. The secret is to use them as a blank canvas. Paint the canvas with your favorite flavors and ingredients, and you will never find oats boring ever again. Get your cereal bowl and your spoon ready, and try the amazing combinations I have gathered here for you.

ALMOND JOY OVERNIGHT OATS

These Almond Joy Overnight Oats are a delicious way to enjoy the flavors of an Almond Joy candy bar, but without any of the guilt or sugar crash. To enhance the flavor of the almonds, add coconut milk and coconut butter. Almond + coconut = a perfect flavor combination. Plus, the added ingredients give you a totally different texture from regular oatmeal.

FOR THE OATS

½ cup (50 g) rolled oats
½ cup (120 ml) unsweetened coconut milk
1 tbsp (10 g) chia seeds
1 tbsp (10 g) coconut butter, melted and cooled
1 tbsp (5 g) dark cocoa powder
1 tbsp (15 ml) pure maple syrup
¼ tsp almond extract

FOR SERVING

1 tbsp (16 g) almond butter
1 tsp dark chocolate chips
1 tsp raw sliced almonds
1 tsp unsweetened shredded coconut

For the oats, place the oats, coconut milk, chia seeds, coconut butter, dark cocoa powder, maple syrup, and almond extract in a mixing bowl. Stir to combine well. Divide the oats into two 8-ounce (240-ml) jars with lids or sealable containers. I use Mason jars.

Refrigerate the oats overnight, or for at least 4 hours. The oats can be enjoyed straight from the refrigerator or can be heated in the microwave for 30 to 60 seconds.

For serving, top the oats with the almond butter, chocolate chips, almonds, and coconut.

Note: Almond Joy Overnight Oats is a great dairy-free and vegan recipe.

BANANAS FOSTER OVERNIGHT OATS

While it is great to simply add banana to oats and call it a day, bananas Foster is definitely better. Because breakfast + dessert is always a good idea, especially when the combination is good for you. To make these oats, cook the bananas first with cinnamon, nutmeg, vanilla extract, and pure maple syrup in a little bit of coconut oil to create a to-die-for, golden, caramelized crust on the bananas. Then, combine the banana mixture with oats and other ingredients and enjoy this breakfast-dessert guilt-free.

FOR THE BANANAS

1 tsp coconut oil
¼ tsp ground cinnamon
⅛ tsp ground nutmeg
2 ripe bananas, sliced
2 tbsp (30 ml) pure maple syrup
1 tsp vanilla extract

FOR THE OATS

1 cup (100 g) rolled oats
1 cup (240 ml) unsweetened almond milk
2 tbsp (30 ml) pure maple syrup
½ tsp ground cinnamon
¼ tsp vanilla extract

For the bananas, heat the coconut oil in a small skillet or saucepan over medium heat. Add the cinnamon and nutmeg to the oil, and swirl to mix together. Add the bananas and cook until they start to break down, 2 to 3 minutes.

Add the maple syrup, stir to combine, and cook for another minute. Remove the pan from the heat. Add the vanilla and stir again.

To make the oats, place the oats, milk, maple syrup, cinnamon, and vanilla in a mixing bowl, and stir to combine. Divide into two 8-ounce (240-ml) jars with lids or sealable containers.

Spoon half of the cooked bananas over each serving of oats.

Refrigerate the oats overnight, or for at least 4 hours. The oats can be enjoyed cold straight from the refrigerator or heated in the microwave for 1 to 2 minutes.

CARAMEL APPLE CINNAMON CRISP OVERNIGHT OATS

These oats are a great dessert-breakfast mix that is incredibly delicious, but good for you, too. It's made clean by cooking the apples using coconut sugar instead of refined white sugar and adding cinnamon and nutmeg for spice. Prep the oats by mixing all the ingredients, then make a date caramel sauce that's healthier than any caramel sauce you can purchase from the grocery store and so luscious that you'll fall in love with it.

FOR THE CINNAMON APPLES

2 large Honeycrisp or Pink Lady apples, cored, peeled, and diced
2 tbsp (20 g) coconut sugar
⅛ tsp cinnamon
⅛ tsp nutmeg

FOR THE OATS

1½ cups (150 g) rolled oats
1½ cups (360 ml) unsweetened almond milk
2 tbsp (20 g) chia seeds
1 tsp vanilla extract
¼ tsp ground cinnamon

FOR THE DATE CARAMEL SAUCE

10–12 pitted dried dates
⅛ tsp sea salt
½ cup (120 ml) hot water, divided

To make the cinnamon apples, combine the apples, coconut sugar, cinnamon, and nutmeg in a saucepan, and cook over medium heat for 6 to 8 minutes, until the apples are softened, but not mushy.

For the oats, combine the oats, milk, chia seeds, vanilla, and cinnamon in a mixing bowl.

To make the date caramel sauce, process the dates and sea salt in a food processor until they are finely chopped. Add the water, 1 tablespoon (15 ml) at a time, to the dates until the mixture becomes smooth and resembles caramel. You may need to scrape down the sides of the food processor.

Spoon half of the oat mixture into the bottom of an 8-ounce (240-ml) jar with a lid or a sealable container, then top with the date sauce and apples. Repeat in a second jar with the remaining ingredients.

Refrigerate the oats overnight, or for at least 4 hours. The oats can be enjoyed cold straight from the refrigerator or heated in the microwave for 1 to 2 minutes.

MAPLE-PECAN BEET OVERNIGHT OATS

Maple-pecan is such an amazing flavor combo. Like all nuts, pecans are packed with good fats and rich in minerals, such as manganese, magnesium, zinc, copper, iron, and potassium.

This recipe combines the amazing flavors of maple-pecan with amazing beets to create such a simple but delicious breakfast. You get all the earthy goodness of beets in your meal without sacrificing flavor, since they go so well with the maple. A Greek yogurt topping sweetened with pure maple syrup and flavored with vanilla brings everything together. Yummy.

FOR THE OATS

2 medium raw beets, peeled and diced

1 cup (240 ml) unsweetened almond milk

2 tbsp (30 ml) pure maple syrup

1 tsp vanilla extract

1 cup (100 g) rolled oats

1 tbsp (10 g) chia seeds

FOR THE MAPLE-PECAN TOPPING

¼ cup (30 g) pecans, plus more for topping

1 tbsp (15 ml) pure maple syrup

½ tsp ground cinnamon

FOR THE GREEK YOGURT TOPPING

⅓ cup (80 g) plain full-fat Greek yogurt

1 tbsp (15 ml) pure maple syrup

¼ tsp vanilla extract

Process the beets, milk, maple syrup, and vanilla in a food processor or blender until smooth.

In a large mixing bowl, combine the oats and chia seeds, and stir to mix well. Add the beet mixture, and stir to combine. Divide the mixture between two 8-ounce (240-ml) jars with lids or sealable containers. Refrigerate overnight, or for at least 4 hours.

For the maple-pecan topping, toast the pecans. Heat a skillet over medium heat, then add the pecans. Cook, tossing frequently, until the pecans turn darker brown and become aromatic, 4 to 6 minutes. Then, add the maple syrup and cinnamon, and stir constantly for 3 to 4 minutes, or until the syrup crystallizes and turns into a powder. Remove the pan from the heat immediately, and allow the nuts to cool. Be careful not to let them burn. Store the topping in an airtight container if you make it ahead.

For the yogurt topping, stir together the yogurt, maple syrup, and vanilla in a small bowl. Refrigerate, covered, if you make it ahead.

To serve, top the refrigerated oats with the yogurt mixture, maple pecans, and raw pecans.

Note: Beets are amazing. They are nutritious, delicious, and they can be used in so many dishes. Beets are low in calories and high in nutrients, including fiber, vitamins, such as B6 and C, and nitrates, which are known to help lower blood pressure. Plus, they make food such a pretty color!

PB&J OVERNIGHT OATS

Seriously, nothing is more comforting than PB&J. It's linked to amazing family memories and so many wonderful moments. This well-loved childhood snack is packed with protein, fiber, and good fats . . . when it's made from whole ingredients, that is!

PB&J Overnight Oats are made with rolled oats, almond milk, peanut butter, chia seeds, fresh raspberries, and maple syrup. No more empty carbs. No more refined sugar. Just the same amazing taste you remember and love.

FOR THE RASPBERRY JAM
2 cups (240 g) fresh raspberries, plus more for topping

2–4 tsp (10–20 ml) pure maple syrup, divided

2–2½ tbsp (20–25 g) chia seeds, divided

FOR THE DIY PEANUT BUTTER
2 cups (295 g) raw, shelled peanuts

⅛ tsp sea salt

FOR THE OATS
2 tbsp (30 ml) pure maple syrup

1½ cups (360 ml) unsweetened almond milk

1½ cups (150 g) rolled oats

2 tbsp (20 g) chia seeds

FOR SERVING
Chopped peanuts, optional

Natural peanut butter, optional

To make the jam, cook the raspberries in a medium saucepan over medium heat until the raspberries break down and release juices, 5 to 10 minutes. Mash the fruit with the back of a spatula or a potato masher, until it reaches your desired texture, lumpy or smooth.

Remove the pan from the heat, and stir in 2 teaspoons (10 ml) of the maple syrup. Taste the jam, and add more of the remaining 2 teaspoons (10 ml) of maple syrup, a teaspoon at a time, if needed for additional sweetness.

Add 2 tablespoons (20 g) of the chia seeds to the jam, and stir to combine. Let the jam stand for 5 to 10 minutes, or until thickened. The jam will continue to thicken, especially after it's refrigerated, but if you'd like thicker jam, stir in the remaining ½ tablespoon (5 g) of chia seeds. Let the jam cool to room temperature, then transfer it to a jar with a lid or sealable container.

To make the peanut butter, preheat your oven to 350°F (180°C), and line a rimmed baking sheet with parchment paper. Add the peanuts to the baking sheet, and roast until they are lightly golden and glossy with oil, 8 to 10 minutes.

Remove the peanuts from the oven, and transfer them to a food processor, along with the salt. Process the nuts for 5 to 6 minutes, stopping to scrape down the sides and bottom of the bowl, as needed. The peanut butter is ready when it is completely smooth.

For the oats, combine ⅓ cup (85 g) of the peanut butter, the maple syrup, and the milk in a mixing bowl. Stir in the oats and chia seeds.

Place about 2 tablespoons (40 g) of the raspberry jam in the bottom of four 8-ounce (240-ml) jars with lids or sealable containers. Pour one-quarter of the peanut butter–oat mixture over the raspberry jam in each jar. Cover and refrigerate overnight, or for at least 4 hours.

For serving, top the oats with the raspberries and, if desired, the chopped peanuts and peanut butter. The oats can be enjoyed cold or heated in the microwave for 1 to 2 minutes.

 Note: Store unused peanut butter in an airtight container at room temperature for up to 1 week or in the fridge for up to 6 months and any unused jam in the refrigerator for up to 2 weeks. The homemade peanut butter and raspberry jam are great on homemade PB&J sandwiches, too! If using a store-bought peanut butter, make sure to find one that contains only peanuts and possibly some salt.

STRAWBERRY SHORTCAKE OVERNIGHT OATS

These overnight oats are easy to make and have the amazing flavor of strawberry shortcake, but none of the unhealthy ingredients. Thanks to the Greek yogurt that is lightly sweetened with raw honey and sweet strawberries, the resulting creamy strawberry texture is dreamy.

1 cup (100 g) rolled oats
1 cup (240 ml) unsweetened almond milk
1 cup (166 g) strawberries, diced, plus more for serving
¼ cup (60 g) plain full-fat Greek yogurt, plus more for serving
2 tsp (14 g) raw honey
½ tsp almond extract
½ tsp vanilla extract

In a small bowl, mix the oats, milk, strawberries, yogurt, honey, almond extract, and vanilla until well combined. Divide the mixture between two 8-ounce (240-ml) jars with lids or sealable containers. Refrigerate overnight, or for at least 4 hours.

When ready to serve, top the oats with additional strawberries and yogurt. The oats can be enjoyed cold or heated in the microwave for 1 to 2 minutes.

TROPICAL SUNRISE OVERNIGHT OATS

If I say tropical sunrise, what's the first thing that goes through your mind? The actual awe-inspiring tropical sunrise or the popular alcoholic drink? Either way, the image you have in your head right now is filled with beautiful colors and the wonderful sensation of a stress-free moment, am I right?

Stress-free breakfasts are kinda my thing. These oats have amazing tropical flavors from mango and pineapple. A tropical, filling breakfast is a wonderful idea, if you ask me. Always. And, when it's in the form of Tropical Sunrise Overnight Oats, it is also quick and easy to make.

FOR THE OATS

1 cup (240 ml) unsweetened coconut milk

1 ripe banana

1 tsp vanilla extract

1 cup (100 g) rolled oats

2 tsp (20 g) chia seeds

½ cup (80 g) diced fresh mango, plus more for topping

¼ cup (42 g) diced fresh pineapple, plus more for topping

FOR SERVING

2 tbsp (10 g) unsweetened shredded coconut

1 tbsp (10 g) raw sliced almonds

For the oats, place the coconut milk, banana, and vanilla in a blender, and blend until smooth.

In a mixing bowl, mix well the oats and chia seeds. Pour the banana mixture into the bowl, and stir to combine. Add the mango and pineapple, and fold in until evenly mixed.

Divide the oat mixture between two 8-ounce (240-ml) jars with lids or sealable containers. Refrigerate overnight, or for at least 4 hours.

For serving, top the oats with the mango, pineapple, coconut, and almonds. Enjoy the oats cold, or heat them in the microwave for 1 to 2 minutes.

Easy
POWER-PACKED SMOOTHIES

Smoothies are so quick and easy to make. They are great for breakfast or a snack, and they are versatile, which means you can adjust them as you want to please your taste.

A smoothie is packed with whole ingredients and is rich in protein, good fats, vitamins, and other nutrients, but not high in sugar. I also love how easy it is to mimic your favorite flavors in a smoothie. Say hello to a decadent raspberry cheesecake (page 68) or a smooth red velvet cake (page 71), all in smoothie form, so you can enjoy it as part of a quick morning routine.

In this chapter, you will discover the world of smoothies and learn how to make smoothies clean by choosing the ingredients wisely and by limiting the amounts of sweeteners. In this way, you'll end up with a tasty and filling smoothie that is good for you and will power you through the day.

CARROT *and* GINGER SMOOTHIE

Carrots are highly nutritious and naturally sweet. They are low in calories and filled with antioxidants; vitamins; such as K, A, and B6; and potassium. Ginger is also a nutritious powerhouse that will bring you numerous health benefits. It has been used for its medicinal purpose for centuries.

This Carrot and Ginger Smoothie might not be the typical fruit-based smoothie, but it's definitely delicious and good for you. To make the smoothie, all you have to do is blend all the ingredients—frozen banana, carrots, fresh ginger, turmeric, coconut milk, and pure maple syrup—in a blender until smooth. Easy, fresh, and colorful.

1 ripe banana, frozen

2 medium carrots, chopped

½" (12-mm) piece ginger

¼ tsp ground turmeric

¾ cup (180 ml) coconut milk, plus more if needed

1 tbsp (15 ml) pure maple syrup

Ice, optional

In a high-speed blender, combine the banana, carrots, ginger, turmeric, coconut milk, and maple syrup. Blend until smooth. If you prefer a thicker consistency, add some ice cubes and blend again. For a thinner consistency, add additional coconut milk.

CHOCOLATE-AVOCADO SMOOTHIE

A chocolate smoothie is a rich and delicious sweet treat that can make your day better. Like any other chocolate dessert, for that matter. This smoothie is rich, creamy, and smooth, and it doesn't contain any processed ingredients. How exciting, right? To make the chocolate smoothie clean, I use unsweetened almond milk, banana, dates, avocado, unsweetened cocoa powder, vanilla extract, and dark chocolate for the topping. This smoothie has the rich and creamy consistency of a regular chocolate smoothie, but it's filled with ingredients that are good for you—good fats from the avocado; fiber, vitamins, and natural sweetness from the dates; and pure chocolate goodness from the cocoa powder and dark chocolate topping. Heck, you can even turn this smoothie into a pudding. Just saying . . .

1¼ cups (300 ml) unsweetened almond milk, plus more if needed

1 ripe banana, frozen

2 pitted dried dates

½ avocado, plus more for topping

2 tbsp (10 g) unsweetened cocoa powder

½ tsp vanilla extract

Shaved dark chocolate, for topping

Combine the almond milk, banana, dates, avocado, cocoa powder, and vanilla in a blender. Blend until smooth. Add more almond milk, as needed, to achieve your desired consistency.

Top the smoothie with the dark chocolate and extra diced avocado.

Note: Turn this Chocolate-Avocado Smoothie into a rich chocolate pudding by reducing the amount of almond milk when blending.

LEMON CLEANSER SMOOTHIE

There's nothing more refreshing than a lemon drink. I love lemonade during the summer. It's fresh and light, and it keeps me hydrated. In fact, lemon is known to promote hydration and to aid with weight loss and digestion, and it is also a great source of vitamin C. More lemon drinks for me, please. Or, why not a lemon smoothie?

For this smoothie, I decided to combine lemon juice with mango, kale, and cucumber. The result? A refreshing smoothie with amazing flavors that will help your body get rid of toxins, improve digestion, help you lose weight, and keep you hydrated. Adding greens and veggies to your smoothies is a great way to consume these nutrient-rich foods when you're not a fan of their taste. The flavor of the greens won't negatively impact the taste of the smoothie if you use ingredients that can easily overpower the taste of the greens. In this case, the lemon, mango, and cucumber flavors are more prominent than that of the kale.

Packed with nutrients, antioxidants, minerals, and vitamins, it's the perfect afternoon snack.

2 cups (135 g) roughly chopped fresh kale, stems removed
2 cups (480 ml) water, plus more if needed
2 cups (330 g) frozen mango chunks
½ cup (60 g) diced cucumber, plus cucumber slices for topping
¼ tsp lemon zest
¼ cup (60 ml) freshly squeezed lemon juice
1 tsp chopped ginger
¼ cup (4 g) fresh cilantro , plus more for topping
Ice, optional

In a high-speed blender, blend the kale and the water together until smooth.

Add the mango, cucumber, lemon zest, lemon juice, ginger, and cilantro. Blend again until the mixture is smooth. Add ice to thicken, if desired, and additional water to thin the smoothie, if needed.

Top the smoothie with the cucumber slices and extra cilantro.

RASPBERRY CHEESECAKE SMOOTHIE

MAKES 2
SERVINGS

To make smoothies clean, one trick you can use is to limit or replace ingredients that are high in sugar with fruits that have lower sugar content.

This smoothie looks like a smoothie, tastes like a delicious cheesecake, and is filling, creamy, smooth, and nutritious. Raspberries are low in calories and sugar, but high in antioxidants and other compounds that promote health. Plus, they are totally delicious and have just the best color, don't you think? To add protein and to make the consistency creamy, I use cottage cheese, but you'd never know it. This Raspberry Cheesecake Smoothie is sweetened with raw honey and flavored with vanilla extract.

1 cup (240 ml) unsweetened coconut milk or milk of choice, plus more if needed

½ cup (105 g) whole milk cottage cheese

2 cups (240 g) frozen or fresh raspberries, plus more frozen for topping

1 tbsp (20 g) raw honey

1½ tsp (8 ml) vanilla extract

Ice, optional

In a high-speed blender, blend the coconut milk, cottage cheese, raspberries, honey, and vanilla until smooth.

If the smoothie is too thin, which is likely if you use fresh raspberries, add ice. If it's too thick, you can thin it with additional coconut milk.

Top the smoothie with the frozen raspberries.

RED VELVET SMOOTHIE

I'm still swooning over this smoothie—you get the amazing flavors of red velvet cake, without the sugar and red food coloring, in a matter of minutes. Plus, it's clean and it contains highly-nutritious ingredients such as almond milk, banana, cherries, beet, almond butter, cocoa powder, and raw honey. I also make a quick and fluffy coconut whipped cream, and top the cream with cocoa nibs. The result is utter red velvet cake perfection. Still swooning over here!

FOR THE SMOOTHIE

1 cup (240 ml) unsweetened almond milk

1 ripe banana, frozen

½ cup (130 g) frozen cherries

1 small beet, raw or cooked

1 tbsp (16 g) almond butter

1 tbsp (5 g) unsweetened cocoa powder

1 tsp raw honey

FOR THE COCONUT WHIPPED CREAM

1 (13.5-oz [400-ml]) can full-fat coconut milk, refrigerated

1 tbsp (15 ml) pure maple syrup

¼ tsp vanilla extract

⅛ tsp sea salt

Cocoa nibs, for topping

For the smoothie, combine the almond milk, banana, cherries, beet, almond butter, cocoa powder, and honey in a blender. Blend until smooth.

Before getting started on the whipped cream, make sure you have refrigerated the coconut milk until it is completely chilled (overnight is best). Scoop out the thick cream at the top of the can, leaving the looser coconut water for another use. In a stand mixer (or a large bowl, if you are using a stick blender or hand blender), place the coconut cream, maple syrup, vanilla, and salt. Using a whisk attachment, beat the cream on high speed until it is fluffy and stiff ridges have formed.

Top the smoothie with the coconut whipped cream and cocoa nibs.

SPICY GREEN MANGO SMOOTHIE

Adding greens to smoothies is a great way to pack more fiber and vitamins into your diet. Spinach is perfect in smoothies. You won't notice the taste, but you will definitely get the health benefits. How wonderful, right?

This smoothie is spicy, sweet, and different. Different in a good way, of course. It has tropical flavors from the banana, mango, and pineapple, a lot of goodness from the spinach, and a little heat from the jalapeño. So refreshing!

FOR THE SMOOTHIE

1 cup (240 ml) unsweetened coconut milk, plus more if needed

½ medium ripe banana, frozen

½ cup (80 g) frozen mango

¼ cup (42 g) frozen pineapple chunks, plus more for topping

1 cup (30 g) fresh spinach

½ jalapeño pepper, seeded and chopped, plus jalapeño slices for topping

1 tsp chopped ginger

¼ tsp ground cinnamon

For the smoothie, use a high-speed blender to blend the coconut milk, banana, mango, pineapple, spinach, jalapeño, ginger, and cinnamon until smooth. If necessary, add additional coconut milk to reach your desired consistency.

Top the smoothie with the cilantro and jalapeño.

Note: To make the Spicy Green Mango Smoothie even spicier, you can add a dash of cayenne pepper, which has been shown to boost metabolism and to lower blood pressure.

STRAWBERRY-ORANGE SUNRISE SMOOTHIE

This smoothie is a balanced choice because it contains fresh fruit and plain full-fat Greek yogurt, which adds protein. Strawberries and oranges are lower in sugar and high in nutritious compounds, such as vitamins and minerals. This creamy smoothie is packed with goodness—and you get it in less than 10 minutes.

1 ripe banana, frozen

1 cup (144 g) strawberries, hulled, plus extra for topping

½ orange, peeled and seeded, plus orange slices for topping

½ cup (120 g) plain full-fat Greek yogurt

Raw honey, optional

Ice, optional

In a high-speed blender, blend the banana, strawberries, orange, and yogurt until the mixture is smooth enough to pour. Taste for sweetness, and add some honey, if needed. Add ice if the smoothie is too thin.

Top the smoothie with a strawberry and an orange slice.

Grab-'N'-Go
MUFFINS AND BREAKFAST BARS

Say yes to muffins and breakfast bars. A big yes!

Contrary to store-bought, packaged snacks, you won't need tons of ingredients to make the delicious breakfast muffins and bars in this chapter. Some of the recipes are sweet, like the addicting Blueberry Cheesecake Breakfast Bars (page 79) and the sneaky Chocolate Zucchini Protein Muffins (page 83), and some are savory, like the Cauliflower Hash Egg Muffins (page 80). Still others are a combination of sweet and savory, like the Jalapeño and Cheddar Cornmeal Muffins (page 87). All of them are amazing and tasty. Your favorite grab-and-go breakfast will no longer be on the do-not-eat list.

Just follow a few basic rules, like replacing all-purpose flour with a more nutritious flour, using fruits and veggies, opting for sugar alternatives, and replacing refined ingredients with clean, whole ingredients, and you're on your way to a high-energy, highly satisfying morning. It's a no brainer, right?

BLUEBERRY CHEESECAKE BREAKFAST BARS

These bars are a clean version of a classic cheesecake, and they're just as rich, satisfying, and dense as you'd expect a cheesecake bar to be. Plus, they're made with clean alternatives to traditional ingredients—for example, the cream cheese is replaced with soaked raw cashews (you won't even know they're in there!), the butter is replaced with coconut oil, the graham cracker crust with a to-die-for nut and oats crust, and the sugar gets nixed for pure maple syrup and dates. Sounds more breakfast-appropriate now, right? These are seriously addicting, I warn you.

FOR THE CHEESECAKE FILLING

1½ cups (210 g) raw cashews

2 cups (480 ml) water, boiled

⅔ cup (160 ml) full-fat coconut milk, refrigerated

Freshly squeezed juice of 2 medium lemons

⅓ cup (75 g) coconut oil, melted

⅓ cup (80 ml) pure maple syrup

1 cup (140 g) fresh blueberries

FOR THE CRUST

1 cup (120 g) raw pecans

12 pitted dried dates

2 tbsp (10 g) rolled oats, plus more for topping

⅛ tsp sea salt

For the filling, cover the cashews with the water and let them soak for a minimum of 1 hour, or up to overnight. It's necessary to soak them to soften them.

Make the crust while the cashews soak. In a food processor or high-speed blender, process the pecans, dates, oats, and salt. The mixture will first be the consistency of cornmeal. Continue to process it until a small ball forms, and then until the mixture resembles a loose dough.

Line a 9 x 5–inch (23 x 12.5–cm) loaf pan or an 8-inch (20-cm) square pan with parchment paper. A pan with shallow sides will make the crust easier to press, but it is not necessary. Carefully pack down the date–pecan mixture evenly, using your fingers.

To continue with the filling, drain the soaked cashews, and place them in a blender. Scoop the hardened coconut milk from the top of the can, leaving the clear liquid underneath (you can save the water for another use, if desired). Add the solid coconut milk, lemon juice, coconut oil, and maple syrup to the blender. Blend the mixture together until very smooth; the smoother this mixture is, the creamier your cheesecake will be. Gently fold in the blueberries, and pour the mixture on top of the prepared crust.

Freeze the mixture in the pan for 1 to 2 hours to allow it to set. When it's solid, remove the bars from the freezer, and cut them into 2-inch (5-cm) squares.

Store the bars in an airtight container in the freezer, separated by parchment paper so they don't stick to each other. To serve the bars, thaw them for 5 minutes at room temperature, so they soften slightly.

Note: Blueberries are low in sugar and calories, and high in nutrients and antioxidants, so they are perfect for a light and nutritious breakfast.

CAULIFLOWER HASH EGG MUFFINS

These Cauliflower Hash Egg Muffins are a healthier, low-calorie alternative to the classic breakfast of hash browns and eggs, and more nutritious, too, because cauliflower is packed with fiber, minerals, and vitamins. Plus, eating muffins for breakfast is always a good idea, especially when the muffins are good for you.

Fortunately, there are ways to make hash browns clean, because they're amazing and need to be in the food rotation. First, use a little bit of olive oil instead of deep-frying, and opt for a healthier, low-carb alternative for potatoes, like cauliflower. Then, turn everything into muffins because it's easier, they are great for a make-ahead breakfast (hello, handheld food!), and the flavors will be better.

½ tbsp (8 ml) olive oil, plus more for greasing the pan

½ cup (70 g) finely diced yellow onion

3 cups (255 g) riced cauliflower (see Note, page 39)

2 egg whites

¼ cup (20 g) grated Parmesan cheese

½ tsp sea salt

¼ tsp ground black pepper

¼ tsp garlic powder

12 eggs

2 green onions, sliced, for garnish

Preheat the oven to 425°F (220°C), and grease a 12-cup muffin pan with olive oil.

Heat the olive oil over medium-high heat in a large skillet. Add the onion, and cook until tender, 4 to 6 minutes. Add the cauliflower, and cook until it becomes slightly tender, 3 to 4 minutes.

Transfer the cauliflower mixture to a large bowl, then add the egg whites, Parmesan, salt, pepper, and garlic powder. Mix well.

Scoop a little less than ¼ cup (21 g) of the cauliflower mixture into each muffin cup. Using your fingers or a spoon, press the cauliflower mixture down and around the sides of the muffin cup to create nests. Bake the nests for 18 to 20 minutes, or until the top edges become golden and crispy.

Reduce the heat to 375°F (190°C), and remove the muffin pan from the oven.

Crack 1 egg into each cup, taking care not to overflow the nest. Return the pan to the oven and bake for 8 to 10 minutes, or until the egg whites are no longer transparent, but still a little loose. For fully cooked-through eggs, bake for 2 to 5 minutes longer.

To serve, garnish the muffins with the green onions. The muffins can be refrigerated, in an airtight container, for up to 5 days. Reheat them in the microwave for 1½ minutes.

CHOCOLATE ZUCCHINI PROTEIN MUFFINS

Chocolate muffins are such a treat. The rich texture and chocolaty taste of chocolate muffins make the perfect option for those who love a sweet breakfast. Plus, chocolate muffins + coffee = perfection. If you use clean ingredients, you can turn chocolate muffins into an amazing low-fat and low-sugar breakfast option. All the bad ingredients are replaced with good ones: butter with coconut oil, sugar with coconut sugar, sweetened cocoa powder with unsweetened cocoa powder, milk chocolate chips with dark chocolate chips, and all-purpose flour with spelt flour. Chocolate protein powder makes the muffins high in protein, and grated zucchini makes them rich in fiber and added nutrients. Don't worry, zucchini won't alter the taste—they will still taste like chocolate muffins . . . but with a secret.

2 tbsp (30 g) coconut oil, melted, plus more for greasing the pan

¼ cup (50 g) coconut sugar

2 eggs

1 cup (255 g) unsweetened applesauce

¼ tsp vanilla extract

1½ cups (149 g) spelt flour

½ cup (38 g) chocolate protein powder (I like Naked Nutrition)

2 tbsp (10 g) unsweetened cocoa powder

2 tsp (12 g) baking soda

1 tsp ground cinnamon

¼ tsp sea salt

2 medium zucchini, shredded

½ cup (90 g) dark chocolate chips, plus more for topping

2 tbsp (10 g) rolled oats

Preheat the oven to 350°F (180°C), and grease a 12-cup muffin pan with coconut oil.

In a large mixing bowl, combine the coconut oil, coconut sugar, eggs, applesauce, and vanilla. Whisk together until blended.

Add the spelt flour, protein powder, cocoa powder, baking soda, cinnamon, and salt. Stir to combine, taking care not to overmix.

Add the zucchini and chocolate chips, and fold them into the mixture until well blended.

Spoon the batter into the muffin cups until each cup is filled almost full. Sprinkle a few dark chocolate chips and some rolled oats on top of each muffin.

Bake the muffins for 14 to 16 minutes, or until they are golden brown on top and a toothpick inserted into the center comes out clean.

Transfer the muffins to a cooling rack to cool completely.

 Note: Check the ingredients labels for your protein powders—they should contain minimal ingredients and no added sweeteners. A great option is the Naked Nutrition brand proteins for 100 percent Grass Fed Pure Whey Protein, Egg White Protein, and/or Yellow Pea Protein.

DENVER OMELET MUFFINS

A Denver omelet, also called a *Western,* is traditionally made with eggs, ham, onions, and green pepper, although some add mushrooms and cheese, too. It's easy to make and delicious. Compared to other breakfast staples, this one is pretty healthy and makes a great balanced meal.

I have nothing against this classic omelet: you can enjoy it as it is without it affecting your clean lifestyle. However, I think a Denver omelet is better in muffin form, don't you?

These muffins are great for make-ahead breakfasts. Make them once and enjoy them every morning without having to cook breakfast every single day. Not only that, but Denver Omelet Muffins are great for portion control. You won't eat more than you should, which you might be tempted to do with the traditional version. Plus, the muffin form is great for a grab-and-go breakfast!

Olive oil, for greasing the pan
½ cup (70 g) diced yellow onion
1 cup (150 g) diced green bell pepper
1 cup (150 g) diced cooked thick-sliced ham
½ cup (55 g) shredded cheddar cheese
8 eggs, beaten
2 egg whites
1 tsp sea salt
½ tsp ground black pepper
¼ tsp garlic powder
2 green onions, sliced, for garnish

Preheat the oven to 350°F (180°C), and lightly grease a 12-cup muffin pan with olive oil.

Divide the onion, pepper, and ham evenly among the muffin cups. Add the cheddar cheese evenly over the top.

In a medium bowl, whisk the eggs, egg whites, salt, pepper, and garlic powder. Pour the mixture over the top of the cheese until the cups are almost full.

Bake the muffins for 20 to 22 minutes, or until the egg is set. Remove the muffins from the oven and serve warm, garnished with the green onions, or let the muffins cool before refrigerating. Store the omelet muffins in an airtight container in the fridge for up to 5 days. To reheat, microwave them for 30 seconds.

JALAPEÑO *and* CHEDDAR CORNMEAL MUFFINS

These muffins are a sweet and savory delight with a little heat from the jalapeño. The jalapeño and cheddar cheese combo is a classic that tastes amazing in general, but is extra special in cornmeal muffins that are great for satisfying cheese cravings. These breakfast muffins are fluffy and soft, and the baked jalapeño tastes heavenly and adds an interesting touch. Making these muffins clean is surprisingly very easy—you'll be using almond flour instead of all-purpose flour, coconut sugar instead of refined white sugar, and coconut oil instead of shortening. Easy!

P.S. You *need* to drizzle these babies with some raw honey to up the flavor—it's unreal!

¼ cup (55 g) coconut oil, melted, plus more for greasing the pan

1 cup (120 g) almond flour

1 cup (160 g) coarse yellow cornmeal

1 tbsp (10 g) coconut sugar

2 tsp (8 g) baking powder

½ tsp sea salt

1 cup (240 ml) unsweetened almond milk

2 eggs

½ cup (55 g) shredded sharp cheddar cheese

1 jalapeño pepper, seeded and minced, plus more for slicing and topping

Raw honey

Preheat the oven to 400°F (200°C), and lightly grease a 12-cup muffin pan with coconut oil.

Place the almond flour, cornmeal, coconut sugar, baking powder, and salt in a large bowl, and whisk to combine.

In a separate mixing bowl, combine the milk, eggs, and coconut oil.

Add the milk mixture to the cornmeal mixture, and stir to mix well. Fold in the cheese and the jalapeño.

Divide the batter among the muffin cups, and top it with a slice of jalapeño.

Bake the muffins until they are golden brown and a toothpick inserted into the center comes out clean, 15 to 20 minutes.

Let the muffins cool briefly in the pan before removing them. To serve, drizzle the muffins with the honey.

SWEET POTATO CASSEROLE MUFFINS

Sweet potato casserole is sweet, dense, and crunchy. It's one of my favorite Thanksgiving sides and it's a dish that can be made clean pretty easily (just check my blog!). Replacing brown sugar with coconut sugar, all-purpose flour with spelt flour, and butter with coconut oil does the trick. It's clean, but still delicious, which is always what I'm going for with my recipes.

While the casserole is an amazing holiday side, why wait for Thanksgiving to enjoy its amazing taste? Turn it into a delicious breakfast you can enjoy any time of the year. Heck, yeah! Introducing Sweet Potato Casserole Muffins. These muffins have the familiar and amazing taste of sweet potato casserole, the same amazing crunchy and sweet pecan topping, and they're made with clean and unrefined ingredients. Hello, goodness!

FOR THE MUFFINS

¼ cup (55 g) coconut oil, softened, plus more for greasing the pan

1½ cups (149 g) spelt flour

½ cup (100 g) coconut sugar

1 tsp baking powder

½ tsp baking soda

1 tsp ground cinnamon

½ tsp ground nutmeg

¼ tsp ground ginger

¼ tsp sea salt

2 eggs

⅓ cup (80 ml) unsweetened almond milk

1 tsp vanilla extract

2 cups (510 g) cooked and mashed sweet potato

FOR THE TOPPING

⅓ cup (36 g) chopped pecans

¼ cup (50 g) coconut sugar

⅓ cup (40 g) almond flour

¼ cup (55 g) coconut oil, melted

1 tsp ground cinnamon

For the muffins, preheat the oven to 350°F (180°C), and grease a 12-cup muffin pan with coconut oil.

In a large mixing bowl, whisk together the spelt flour, coconut sugar, baking powder, baking soda, cinnamon, nutmeg, ginger, and salt.

In a separate bowl, whisk together the eggs, coconut oil, milk, vanilla, and sweet potato.

Add the egg mixture to the flour mixture, and stir until just combined. Divide the batter evenly among the muffin cups, filling each about three-quarters full.

For the topping, in a small bowl, combine the pecans, coconut sugar, almond flour, coconut oil, and ground cinnamon. Mix well to incorporate all the flour.

Sprinkle the topping generously and equally over all the muffins.

Bake the muffins for 20 to 22 minutes, or until a toothpick inserted into the center comes out clean. Let the muffins cool in the pan for 5 minutes, then serve, or transfer them to a wire rack to cool completely.

The muffins may be stored in an airtight container for up to 5 days.

DARK CHOCOLATE *and* SEA SALT ENERGY BARS

Is there seriously a better combination of flavors than dark chocolate and sea salt? The rich, salty, bitter, and sweet experience makes me swoon! If you're right there swooning with me, I know you're gonna love these energy bars. They're packed full of natural goodness, including fiber, vitamins, and protein to provide you with nutrients and energy to start your day—all without the high price tag of a store-bought natural energy bar. Plus, they couldn't be easier to make!

Trust me, it will make your morning to open the fridge, grab one of these babies, and be on your merry, dark-chocolate-and-sea-salt way!

1 cup (140 g) raw almonds
1 cup (140 g) raw cashews
24 pitted medjool dates
1¼ cups (95 g) whey protein powder or egg white (I like Naked Nutrition)
¼ cup (20 g) unsweetened cocoa powder
¼–⅓ cup (60–80 ml) unsweetened almond milk
½ tsp coarse sea salt

Line an 8-inch (20-cm) square pan with parchment paper, making sure that some of the parchment paper is overlapping on the sides, so you can use it to pull the mixture out of the pan.

In a food processor, combine the almonds, cashews, and dates, and process until the nuts are chopped. Add the protein powder and cocoa powder, and process again until the dates are broken down. Add ¼ cup (60 ml) of the almond milk, and process until the mixture begins to stick to itself and form a ball. Add more of the remaining 1 tablespoon (15 ml) of almond milk, a little at a time, if needed for the ball to form.

Transfer the mixture to the prepared baking dish, and press the mixture out as evenly as possible using your hands. Then, using an additional sheet of parchment paper on top, press the mixture out even more, until it's as smooth and even as possible. Using the bottom of a glass as a small, makeshift rolling pin can help.

Sprinkle the salt evenly over the top of the mixture, and then gently press to make the salt stick.

Refrigerate the bars for 30 to 60 minutes, or until they are set and mostly solid. Then, remove the bars by pulling the parchment paper up from the baking dish. Cut into 12 to 16 even bars.

Store the bars in an airtight container in the refrigerator between layers of parchment paper, to keep the bars from sticking to each other.

Note: These bars can be wrapped and stored individually, for easy grab-and-go breakfasts.

Fun Breakfasts
FOR YOUR INNER CHILD

Do you remember what it was like to wake up in the morning with not a care in the world? To be happy, energetic, and entirely stress-free in the morning? It's a very faded memory, right? Oh, childhood, those were the days.

Can we also take a moment to remember the amazing breakfast food we had back in the day? Well, I guess I should say amazing in terms of taste and flavor, not in terms of clean and healthy. I used to love a sugary breakfast. Sugary cereals and Pop-Tarts were among my favorite breakfast foods, along with donuts and cinnamon rolls. So many sweets, and with so little nutritional value!

Health food was definitely not something I stressed about during childhood. Worries about clean food began when I started to gain weight in college and to lose energy. When I was a kid, though, the more sweet treats there were around, the merrier. As adults, our metabolisms are so different, and we have to pay attention to what we eat if we want to be healthy, feel nourished, and have energy.

In this chapter, we will bring back the tastes of childhood, but in a much more reasonable way. We'll get to enjoy Pop-Tarts (page 95), cinnamon rolls (page 97), and donuts (page 98) again, but without the empty calories and sugar crashes. You'll be able to enjoy your favorite treats and sweets from childhood, but maintain your clean-eating lifestyle. It is not only possible, it is also fun, and, of course, incredibly tasty.

HOMEMADE STRAWBERRY POP-TARTS

These Pop-Tarts are so fun! It's probably no surprise that store-bought Pop-Tarts are high in empty calories, high fructose corn syrup and other manufactured sugars, bad fats, plus tons of processed ingredients. My Pop-Tarts have the same flaky, crunchy, and doughy crust—and awesome strawberry filling—but they are actually nutritious.

They make a great breakfast option for those who want to be able to enjoy a sweet, dessert-like breakfast without compromising their health. Say goodbye to artificial colors and flavors with this childhood favorite, and say hello to natural goodness!

FOR THE CRUST

¾ cup (72 g) whole wheat pastry flour
½ cup (50 g) spelt flour
2 tsp (6 g) coconut sugar
½ tsp sea salt
½ cup (110 g) coconut oil, frozen and chopped into small pieces
6–8 tbsp (90–120 ml) ice cold water, divided
1 egg, beaten

FOR THE STRAWBERRY JAM FILLING

2 cups (330 g) diced fresh strawberries
2–4 tsp (14–28 g) raw honey or (15–30 ml) maple syrup
2–2½ tbsp (20–25 g) chia seeds

To make the crust, process the whole wheat pastry flour, spelt flour, coconut sugar, and salt in a food processor, until it's mixed well.

Add the coconut oil, and process until it is broken down into the size of peas.

Add the cold water, 1 tablespoon (15 ml) at a time, to the flour mixture, and pulse the food processor until the dough starts to come together. Use your hands to shape the dough into a disc. Cover it with plastic wrap and refrigerate it for at least 30 minutes, or until it is hard enough to hold together when it's rolled out.

While the dough is chilling, prepare the jam. In a large saucepan over medium heat, cook the strawberries until they break down and release juices, 5 to 10 minutes.

Mash the fruit with the back of a spatula or a potato masher, leaving the texture of the jam lumpy or mashing it until smooth, as you prefer.

Remove the pan from the heat, and stir in 2 teaspoons (14 g) of the honey. Taste, and add the remaining 2 teaspoons (14 g) of honey if it's needed for sweetness.

Add 2 tablespoons (20 g) of the chia seeds to the pan, and stir them in. Let the jam stand for 5 to 10 minutes, or until thickened. The jam will continue to thicken after it's refrigerated, but if you'd like a thicker consistency, stir in the remaining ½ tablespoon (5 g) of chia seeds. Once the jam has cooled to room temperature, transfer it to a jar with a lid or sealable container.

To make the tarts, remove the dough from the fridge about 10 minutes before you want to use it, so it softens just slightly.

On a lightly floured surface, use a rolling pin to roll the dough into a rectangle ⅛ inch (4 mm) thick. Cut smaller rectangles to the size you want your tarts to be— I like 3 x 5 inches (7.5 x 12.5 cm). Reroll the scraps and cut more rectangles.

Use a pastry brush to brush the egg lightly over the pieces of dough. Spread about 2 tablespoons (40 g) of the strawberry jam filling on half of the rectangles, leaving a ½-inch (12-mm) border. Top each jam-covered rectangle with a second piece. With the tines of a fork, press the sides of each tart together, then poke some holes on the top to allow air to escape while baking.

(CONTINUED)

HOMEMADE STRAWBERRY POP-TARTS (CONTINUED)

FOR THE GLAZE
⅓ cup (80 g) plain full-fat Greek yogurt
1 tbsp (15 ml) pure maple syrup
¼ tsp vanilla extract
¼ tsp beet powder, for coloring, optional

Place the tarts on a baking sheet, and refrigerate them for at least 30 minutes or up to 2 hours.

Preheat the oven to 350°F (180°C). Bake the tarts until they are golden brown, about 20 minutes.

Make the glaze while the tarts are cooling from the oven. Whisk together the yogurt, maple syrup, vanilla, and beet powder, if desired. Spread the glaze evenly over the tarts.

 Note: Pop-Tarts are great make-ahead treats. You can make the dough ahead and refrigerate it for up to 3 days. The strawberry jam filling can be refrigerated for up to 7 days. You can also freeze some or all of the assembled tarts before baking them. After pressing the tarts together and poking holes in the tops, wrap the tarts tightly in aluminum foil, and freeze them for up to 4 weeks. Bake frozen tarts for 35 to 40 minutes.

IMPOSSIBLE CINNAMON ROLLS

I call these Impossible Cinnamon Rolls because, when you eat them, it will feel like it's impossible that they are actually good for you! They're the perfect baked treat—fluffy, sweet, gooey, cinnamony, and topped with a delicious thick and creamy frosting. They are *everything*! And they taste so good. Plus, you can eat them for breakfast and brunch, as an after-dinner dessert, or as an afternoon treat with a cup of coffee.

FOR THE DOUGH

1 cup (240 ml) unsweetened almond milk

3 tbsp (40 g) coconut oil, plus more for greasing the pan

1 tbsp (10 g) coconut sugar

1 (2¼-tsp [9-g]) packet instant yeast or rapid-rise yeast

¼ tsp sea salt

2½–3 cups (240–288 g) whole wheat pastry flour, divided

FOR THE FILLING

⅓ cup (65 g) coconut sugar

1½ tbsp (12 g) ground cinnamon

3 tbsp (40 g) coconut oil, melted

2 tbsp (30 ml) pure maple syrup

FOR THE FROSTING

1½ cups (360 g) plain full-fat Greek yogurt

2½ tbsp (38 ml) pure maple syrup

1 tsp vanilla extract

½ tsp maple extract

See photo on page 92.

For the dough, in a large saucepan, heat the almond milk, coconut oil, and coconut sugar until warm and melted, but not boiling. Remove the mixture from the heat, and let it cool for 5 minutes. Transfer the milk mixture to a large mixing bowl, and sprinkle the yeast across the surface. Let it stand for 10 minutes to allow the yeast to activate.

Add the salt and ½ cup (48 g) of the flour to the bowl, and stir it in. Continue to add the remaining flour, ½ cup (48 g) at a time, stirring as you go. The dough will be sticky. When the dough is too thick to stir, transfer it to a lightly floured surface, and knead it for a minute or so, until it forms a loose ball (be careful not to overmix). Continue to add flour a little at a time, as needed, until the dough no longer sticks to your hands. You may not need all of the flour. Knead the dough for 5 minutes, or until all the flour is incorporated and the dough is smooth and springy.

Return the dough to the bowl, cover it with plastic wrap or a clean dish towel, and set it in a warm place to rise for about 1 hour, or until it is doubled in size.

For the filling, combine the coconut sugar and cinnamon in a small bowl. In a separate small bowl, combine the coconut oil and the maple syrup. Set aside the bowls.

Grease an 8-inch (20-cm) square pan with coconut oil.

On a lightly floured surface, roll out the dough into a thin, even ¼-inch (6-mm) rectangle. Brush with the coconut oil and maple syrup mixture. Then, generously sprinkle with the coconut sugar and cinnamon mixture.

Starting at one end, tightly roll up the dough and situate it seam side down. With a serrated knife, cut the dough into ten 1- to 1½-inch (2.5- to 4-cm) sections. Arrange the rolls in the prepared pan.

Let the rolls rise while you preheat the oven to 350°F (180°C).

Once the oven is hot, bake the rolls for 18 to 20 minutes, or until very slightly golden brown. Pay close attention so they do not overcook and get too dry. Allow the rolls to cool in the pan for 10 minutes. Prepare the frosting while the rolls are cooling. Stir together the yogurt, maple syrup, vanilla, and maple extract. Spread the frosting on top of the rolls.

Note: Be sure to store these rolls in the refrigerator, because the frosting is made with Greek yogurt that needs to remain refrigerated. Warm the rolls in the microwave oven for 20 to 30 seconds.

FLOURLESS MAPLE-GLAZED VANILLA BAKED DONUTS *with* PISTACHIO CRUMBLES

Donuts are like the ultimate junk food, right? I mean, c'mon, they are fried dough topped with sugar and sometimes filled with sugar, too! They have little to no nutritional value and will likely make you feel gross after you eat them. Yet, they're amazing and I'll take two more!

In the past, the donuts I enjoyed weren't clean-eating approved, but I still love donuts—eating clean didn't change that for me. What it did change is how I enjoy my donuts. I learned to make them at home using clean ingredients, which means my afternoon sweet treat is now nutritious.

These donuts are topped with a dreamy maple glaze that is sweet and has wonderful coconut, vanilla, and cinnamon flavors. Plus, the donuts get crunch and flavor from the pistachio crumbles. Even my kiddos can't get enough of these!

FOR THE BAKED DONUTS
3 tbsp (40 g) coconut oil, melted and cooled, plus more for greasing the pan
1 cup (120 g) almond flour
¼ cup (32 g) coconut flour
1 tbsp (10 g) arrowroot starch
½ tsp baking soda
¼ tsp sea salt
¼ tsp ground cinnamon
3 eggs
⅓ cup (80 ml) pure maple syrup
¼ cup (60 ml) unsweetened almond milk
1 tsp vanilla extract

FOR THE MAPLE GLAZE
2 tbsp (20 g) coconut butter
1 tbsp (15 g) coconut oil, melted and cooled
2 tbsp (30 ml) pure maple syrup
½ tsp vanilla extract
½ cup (62 g) raw pistachios, crushed
¼ tsp ground cinnamon

For the donuts, grease a donut pan with coconut oil, and preheat the oven to 350°F (180°C). Have ready a cooling rack set into a rimmed baking sheet.

In a large mixing bowl, whisk together the almond flour, coconut flour, arrowroot starch, baking soda, salt, and cinnamon.

In another mixing bowl, whisk together the eggs, maple syrup, coconut oil, almond milk, and vanilla.

Pour the milk mixture into the flour mixture, and stir until fully incorporated, taking care not to overmix.

Using a piping bag, ziplock bag with a corner cut off, or a spoon, pour the mixture into the donut-pan cavities until they're about three-quarters full.

Gently tap the pan to release any air bubbles and smooth out the dough. Bake the donuts for 20 to 24 minutes, or until they're golden and a toothpick inserted into the center comes out clean.

Let the donuts sit in the pan for 5 minutes, then transfer them to the prepared cooling rack.

Prepare the glaze when the donuts are cooled. Mix the coconut butter, coconut oil, maple syrup, and vanilla in a heat-safe bowl and microwave in 20-second increments until it's smooth. You can also heat the glaze in a double boiler.

One at a time, dip each donut into the glaze using a twisting motion, and then return the donut to the rack, glazed side up. Sprinkle the glaze with the pistachios and cinnamon, and let the donuts stand until the glaze is hard, about 5 minutes.

PEANUT BUTTER CRUNCH CEREAL

Peanut Butter Crunch was my absolute favorite cereal growing up. I could eat the stuff all day long. Sadly, store-bought cereal is filled with sugar and high in carbs and calories. I was so excited when I figured out how to make my beloved childhood cereal using unrefined ingredients!

This cereal makes a fun breakfast that's clean at the same time. Not to mention that it tastes better than store-bought and won't leave you feeling tired after your inevitable sugar crash! It's also shockingly simple to make—just mix the clean ingredients, form the balls, and bake them in the oven. Then you can enjoy the world's easiest breakfast every morning of the week without worrying about your sugar and calorie intake.

1⅔ cups (430 g) natural peanut butter

½ cup (100 g) coconut sugar

2 tsp (10 g) coconut oil, melted

½ cup (120 ml) unsweetened almond milk

¼ tsp sea salt

1 tsp vanilla extract

1½ tsp (9 g) baking soda

1 cup (96 g) whole wheat pastry flour

Preheat the oven to 350°F (180°C), and line a cookie sheet with parchment paper.

Combine the peanut butter, coconut sugar, and coconut oil in a large mixing bowl. This should be a thick, but creamy and smooth, mixture. If the mixture is too thick, dry, and not smooth, you can transfer it to a saucepan to loosen it over medium heat.

Add the almond milk, salt, vanilla, and baking soda, and stir to combine. (If you heated the mixture to loosen it, transfer it back to the mixing bowl for this step.)

Slowly add in the flour, ½ cup (48 g) at a time, until the dough becomes stiff like cookie dough and holds together, but is easily breakable. Use only enough flour to produce a dough that rolls into balls without being too sticky or crumbly.

Transfer the batter to a pastry bag fitted with a ¼-inch (6-mm) round tip. Holding the bag vertically, close to the baking sheet, pipe ¼-inch (6-mm) balls, leaving some space between each. Use a wet knife to cut each ball in half. You can also use a ⅛-teaspoon measuring spoon, then roll each portion into balls with your hands. Keep the balls separated, so they don't stick together.

Depending on the size of your cookie sheet, you might have to make two batches. Bake the balls for 8 to 10 minutes, depending on the size of the balls. The cereal is ready to be removed from the oven when it has grown slightly in size and has darkened in color. Let the cereal cool on the pan for 10 minutes, then remove from the pan to cool completely. The cereal will become harder as it cools. The cereal may be stored at room temperature in an airtight container for 2 weeks.

PEANUT BUTTER CHOCOLATE CHIP COOKIE DOUGH

OK, so we were always told as kids not to eat the cookie dough—even though that was the best part of making cookies. To this day, I love the taste of cookie dough. Sometimes I feel like I love the cookie dough more than I love actual baked cookies. So, let's enjoy this edible cookie dough that is made with chickpeas and has no eggs or flour, which is what makes regular cookie dough unsafe to eat. Yep, instead it's clean, and it's packed with nutrients and goodness. Oh—and it's one heck of an awesome breakfast!

You can roll the dough into balls and wrap them individually for a quick grab-and-go breakfast.

1 (15-oz [425-g]) can chickpeas with no salt added, drained, rinsed, and patted dry

½ cup (120 g) natural peanut butter

2 tsp (10 ml) vanilla extract

2½ tbsp (38 ml) pure maple syrup

2 tbsp (10 g) rolled oats

½ tsp ground cinnamon

⅛ tsp sea salt

1–2 tbsp (15–30 ml) unsweetened almond milk, divided

⅓ cup (60 g) dark chocolate chips

Place the chickpeas, peanut butter, vanilla, maple syrup, oats, cinnamon, salt, and 1 tablespoon (15 ml) of the milk in a food processor.

Blend the mixture until it is smooth and creamy. If it is too thick, add some or all of the remaining tablespoon (15 ml) of milk to achieve cookie-dough texture.

Transfer the cookie dough to a mixing bowl, and fold in the chocolate chips. Refrigerate the cookie dough in an airtight container for up to 5 days.

Classic
COMFORT FOOD MADE CLEAN

When people think they need to start eating healthy, one of their biggest misconceptions is that they need to give up the foods they love. They worry about how they'll never be able to enjoy a cheeseburger again, or a slice of pizza, or another favorite.

This concern can even keep people away from making better health choices, as the fear of giving up one's comfort food is real and scary.

And why wouldn't it be? Comfort food is amazing. Comfort food reminds us of good memories, our childhoods, places we've lived or visited, and times we've laughed and felt at home. These experiences are real, and so tied to the foods we eat that we go back to the memories time and time again.

The good news is that, with clean eating, you don't have to give up your comfort food. In fact, you'll likely find you get to enjoy more of your comfort foods more often! How is this possible? Well, the trick is to find new ways to enjoy the foods you love. That means replacing bad ingredients, such as refined sugars, processed flours, and artificial ingredients, with whole, unrefined, and nutritious ingredients.

Sounds easy enough, right? It actually is!

In this chapter, we'll dive into some of the common comfort foods many of us know and love—foods like burgers, pizza, nachos, and more. I'll show you which ingredients to switch out and which to include, so your comfort food tastes great, gives you all the same feels, and helps keep you eating clean.

BLACK BEAN BURGERS *with* BAKED CHILI SWEET POTATO WEDGE FRIES

There isn't much more satisfying than biting into a big, juicy, flavorful burger. This black bean burger recipe does not disappoint!

Try swapping this flavorful black bean patty for a beef patty for some added fiber. Ditch the bun in favor of a few crisp iceberg lettuce leaves, for a mighty crunch and to remove unnecessary refined sugars and flours found in regular hamburger buns. Then, use the chipotle yogurt spread instead of cheese and mayo for a punch of spice and tart creaminess that perfectly balances out the savory black bean patty. So good *and* good for you!

FOR THE SWEET POTATO WEDGE FRIES

2 sweet potatoes, cut into wedges

1 tbsp (15 ml) olive oil

1 tsp chili powder

½ tsp sea salt

½ tsp paprika

¼ tsp ground cumin

¼ tsp cayenne pepper

¼ tsp garlic powder

1 tbsp (3 g) chopped fresh Italian parsley, for garnish

FOR THE BLACK BEAN BURGERS

1 (15-oz [425-g]) can black beans with no salt added, drained and rinsed

½ cup (70 g) finely diced red onion

3 green onions, sliced

2 cloves garlic, minced

1 egg

½ cup (60 g) almond flour

½ tsp lime zest

1 tbsp (15 ml) freshly squeezed lime juice

1 tsp sea salt

1 tsp chili powder

1 tsp ground cumin

½ tsp ground black pepper

1 tbsp (15 ml) olive oil

To make the sweet potato wedge fries, preheat your oven to 450°F (230°C), and line a rimmed baking sheet with parchment paper.

On the baking sheet, toss the sweet potatoes, olive oil, chili powder, salt, paprika, cumin, cayenne, and garlic powder, until the potatoes are coated well. Arrange the wedges in a single layer on the baking sheet, and bake them for 20 to 25 minutes, tossing halfway through, until the wedges are crispy on the outside and tender on the inside. Remove the potatoes from the oven, and garnish with the parsley.

Make the black bean burgers while the sweet potatoes are in the oven. In a large mixing bowl, use a potato masher to mash the beans. The beans should be roughly mashed, not fully pureed. Add the red onion, green onions, garlic, egg, almond flour, lime zest, lime juice, salt, chili powder, cumin, and pepper, and stir to combine.

Divide the mixture into four portions, and use your hands to shape each portion into a patty. If the bean mixture is too crumbly to work with, refrigerate it for 20 minutes to firm it and make it easier to form into patties.

Heat the olive oil over medium-high heat in a large skillet. Once the oil is hot, gently place the patties into the hot pan, and cook them for 4 to 6 minutes per side, until a golden crust forms and the patty is heated through. Reshape the patties using your spatula, as needed.

(CONTINUED)

BLACK BEAN BURGERS *with* BAKED CHILI SWEET POTATO WEDGE FRIES (CONTINUED)

FOR THE CHIPOTLE YOGURT SPREAD
½ cup (120 g) plain full-fat Greek yogurt
1 tbsp (15 ml) freshly squeezed lime juice
½ canned chipotle pepper in adobo sauce, minced
½ tsp chili powder
½ tsp paprika
¼ tsp sea salt
¼ tsp garlic powder

FOR SERVING
1 head iceberg lettuce, broken into leaves
1 tomato, sliced
1 red onion, thinly sliced
1 avocado, sliced

Prepare the chipotle yogurt spread while the patties are cooking. Combine the yogurt, lime juice, chipotle pepper, chili powder, paprika, salt, and garlic powder in a small bowl, and mix until smooth. Refrigerate the spread until you are ready to use it.

For serving, spread some of the chipotle spread inside 8 lettuce leaves.

Put a black bean burger on one of the prepared lettuce leaves, followed by the tomato, onion, and avocado. Top with another of the chipotle-lined lettuce leaves, then repeat with the remaining ingredients. Serve with the sweet potato wedge fries. You can use the extra yogurt spread for dipping sauce for the fries, if desired.

SHEET-PAN STEAK FAJITA *and* SWEET POTATO NACHOS

You had me at steak. I mean fajita. I mean sweet potato. I mean nachos. Oh my, so much yumminess and comfort food packed onto one easy baking sheet, so you know the prep and cleanup are gonna be super-fast and easy. These sheet-pan nachos are not for the faint of heart. We've got all the goods you know and love, piled high. The baked sweet potato chips are a great clean alternative to regular tortilla chips, which are typically fried in highly processed oils and then loaded with salt and chemical-like ingredients.

Instead, enjoy all the fiber and nutrients from the spicy sweet potatoes, the fresh and vibrant bell peppers and onions, the lean protein from the perfectly cooked steak, marinated in an easy fajita marinade without any added sugar, the creamy diced avocado, a tart and cool Greek yogurt drizzle with a hint of fresh lime, and just a touch of shredded Monterey Jack cheese. These nachos are so loaded, you'll definitely need a fork to enjoy them!

FOR THE STEAK
1 lb (455 g) flank steak
⅓ cup (80 ml) freshly squeezed lime juice
¼ cup (60 ml) no-sugar-added pineapple juice
2 tbsp (30 ml) low-sodium soy sauce
2 tbsp (30 ml) olive oil, divided
1 clove garlic, minced
1 tsp ground cumin
½ tsp crushed red pepper flakes
¼ cup (4 g) chopped fresh cilantro

FOR THE SWEET POTATO CHIPS
2 large sweet potatoes
1 tbsp (15 ml) olive oil
1 tsp paprika
½ tsp sea salt
¼ tsp garlic powder
¼ tsp ground black pepper

FOR THE FAJITA BELL PEPPERS
1 white onion, sliced
1 poblano chile, sliced
1 red bell pepper, sliced
1 green bell pepper, sliced
1 tsp sea salt
½ tsp ground black pepper
¼ tsp cayenne pepper

For the steak, in a large resealable bag or refrigerator-safe storage container, place the steak, lime juice, pineapple juice, soy sauce, 1 tablespoon (15 ml) of the olive oil, the garlic, cumin, crushed red pepper flakes, and cilantro. Seal the bag tightly to ensure no leakage, and then marinate the steak in the refrigerator for a minimum of 20 minutes, or up to 8 hours.

Prepare the sweet potato chips while the steak is marinating. Preheat your oven to 400°F (200°C), and line a rimmed baking sheet with parchment paper.

Slice the sweet potatoes into ¼-inch (6-mm) slices using either a mandoline or a sharp knife. In a large bowl, add the sliced potatoes, olive oil, paprika, salt, garlic powder, and black pepper, and toss to coat evenly. Place the slices on the baking sheet, taking care not to overcrowd them as much as possible. Bake the potatoes for 15 minutes, flip them, and bake for another 12 to 15 minutes, or until the sweet potato chips are browned and crispy around the edges and beginning to curl upward. Remove the potatoes from the oven, and reduce the temperature to 350°F (180°C).

In a large skillet, heat the remaining 1 tablespoon (15 ml) of the olive oil for the steak over medium-high heat. Add the steak, and cook for 6 to 8 minutes per side, until golden brown on all sides, but not fully cooked through. Remove the steak from the heat, slice it into strips, and set aside.

For the fajita veggies, in the same pan you cooked the steak, quickly toss the onion, poblano chile, red and green bell peppers, salt, black pepper, and cayenne pepper for 3 to 4 minutes, until the veggies just start to soften, but are not fully tender.

(CONTINUED)

SHEET-PAN STEAK FAJITA *and* SWEET POTATO NACHOS (CONTINUED)

FOR THE NACHO TOPPINGS

½ cup (130 g) black beans

½ cup (55 g) shredded Jack cheese

1 avocado, diced

2 tbsp (2 g) chopped fresh cilantro

½ jalapeño pepper, seeded and sliced

3 tbsp (45 g) plain full-fat Greek yogurt

For the nachos, spread the beans over the sweet potato chips on the baking sheet. Then add the fajita veggies, steak, and the cheese.

Cook the nachos, uncovered, in the oven for 6 to 8 minutes, or until the cheese has melted and the beans have been heated through.

To serve, top the nachos with the avocado, cilantro, jalapeño, and a dollop of Greek yogurt.

Note: If you want to jazz up the yogurt and make it a drizzle, mix it with 3 tablespoons (45 ml) of lime juice and ¼ teaspoon of sea salt.

GROWN-UP FISH STICKS *with* HOMEMADE TARTAR SAUCE

Fish sticks: kids love them but—face it—we adults have to admit we love them, too. While convenient and easy to cook, store-bought fish sticks are far from good for you. They are covered with low-nutrient breading, deep-fried, and made with processed ingredients, including fats and even sugar. Yuck. Even the best ones are not very nutritious. My kids love them but, since I embraced a clean lifestyle, I can't get on board with them anymore. However, my husband and I love fish, and so do our kids. So, these Grown-Up Fish Sticks with Homemade Tartar Sauce had to happen in my house. And we are all so glad they did.

These fish sticks are beyond delicious—they'll satisfy your grown-up tastes, but they're still kid-approved, which means they make a perfect family meal everyone can enjoy!

FOR THE FISH STICKS
2 lb (910 g) skinless cod fillet
¼ tsp sea salt
¼ tsp ground black pepper

FOR THE COATING
⅔ cup (57 g) chickpea flour (aka garbanzo bean flour)
½ tsp sea salt
2 eggs
1 cup (120 g) almond flour
½ tsp garlic powder

FOR THE TARTAR SAUCE
¼ cup (60 g) plain full-fat Greek yogurt
1 tbsp (10 g) finely diced dill pickles
1 tbsp (15 g) Dijon mustard
1 tsp freshly squeezed lemon juice
½ tsp chopped fresh dill
⅛ tsp sea salt
⅛ tsp garlic powder

For the fish sticks, preheat the oven to 400°F (200°C), and line a rimmed baking sheet with parchment paper.

Cut the cod into four 2 x 3–inch (5 x 8–cm) long slices to make the sticks. Season the fish with the salt and pepper.

For the coating, you'll need three shallow bowls. In the first bowl, combine the chickpea flour and salt. In the second bowl, beat the eggs. In the third bowl, mix the almond flour and garlic powder. Dredge each cod piece in the chickpea flour mixture to coat completely. Then, dip it into the egg, followed by the almond flour mixture. It is helpful to use one hand for the wet dipping and the other hand for the dry dipping, so your fingers don't also get coated.

Place the cod about 2 inches (5 cm) apart on the prepared baking sheet, and bake for 12 to 14 minutes, or until the cod is cooked through and flaky. Flip the sticks halfway through the baking time.

Make the tartar sauce while the fish is baking. In a medium mixing bowl, stir together the yogurt, pickles, mustard, lemon juice, dill, salt, and garlic powder.

Note: These fish sticks reheat very well in the microwave and are great for meal prep. Make sure to refrigerate the sauce and the fish sticks separately.

NOT-YOUR-CHILDHOOD BEAN *and* RICE BURRITO

Bean and rice burritos are hearty, quick, and easy to make. These zesty burritos are made with cilantro-lime brown rice, spicy black beans, my go-to fresh pico de gallo salsa, and other savory seasonings that make them so much better than the ones I remember from my childhood. And so much healthier, too. Now we're talking.

Wrap up these babies whenever you want to experience the familiar taste of burritos with a delicious upgrade.

FOR THE PICO DE GALLO SALSA

2 large tomatoes, diced

½ small red onion, diced

⅓ cup (5 g) roughly chopped fresh cilantro

1 jalapeño pepper, seeded and finely chopped

1 clove garlic, minced

1 tbsp (15 ml) freshly squeezed lime juice

⅛ tsp sea salt

⅛ tsp ground black pepper

⅛ tsp ground cumin

FOR THE CILANTRO-LIME RICE

1 cup (185 g) brown rice

2 cups (480 ml) low-sodium vegetable broth

2 tbsp (2 g) chopped fresh cilantro

Juice of 1 lime

⅛ tsp sea salt

FOR THE SPICY BLACK BEANS

1 tbsp (15 ml) olive oil

½ small red onion, finely diced

2 cloves garlic, minced

1 jalapeño pepper, seeded and minced

1 (15-oz [425-g]) can black beans with no salt added, drained and rinsed

1 tsp chili powder

½ tsp ground cumin

½ tsp sea salt

FOR THE BURRITOS

4 large cassava flour tortillas or whole-grain wraps

Shredded cheese, optional

Salsa, optional

Avocado slices, optional

Plain full-fat Greek yogurt, optional

To make the pico de gallo, in a large mixing bowl, combine the tomatoes, onion, cilantro, jalapeño, garlic, lime juice, salt, pepper, and cumin. Refrigerate for about 30 minutes to allow the flavors to meld.

For the rice, bring the rice and vegetable broth to a boil over high heat in a medium saucepan with a tight-fitting lid. Reduce the heat to a simmer, and simmer the rice for 30 to 40 minutes, or until it's tender. Let the rice stand for 10 minutes, covered, then fluff it with a fork. Remove 2 cups (390 g) of the rice from the pan, and place it in a large mixing bowl. Add the cilantro, lime juice, and salt to the bowl, and toss to combine.

For the beans, heat the olive oil in a large skillet over medium-high heat. Add the onion, garlic, and jalapeño, and cook, stirring occasionally, for 6 to 8 minutes, or until the onion is tender.

Add the beans, chili powder, cumin, and salt to the skillet, and stir to combine. Cook until heated through, 4 to 6 minutes.

For the burritos, warm the tortillas by wrapping them in a paper towel and microwaving them for 10 to 20 seconds, until they are pliable. You can also briefly heat them over high heat in an ungreased skillet. Spread one-quarter of the beans and rice onto each tortilla. Add the cheese, salsa, avocado, and yogurt, if desired. Fold up opposite sides of the tortilla, and then the bottom, and roll up to enclose the filling. Wrap the burritos in aluminum foil or parchment paper to keep them from opening.

Note: To prep this meal ahead of time, refrigerate the rice, beans, and salsa separately, and then assemble the burritos when you are ready to enjoy them.

QUICK BBQ CHICKEN PITA PIZZAS

Any excuse I can get to enjoy BBQ chicken and pizza, I'm there. There's something about the deep, sweet flavors of a good BBQ sauce mixed with tender chicken that makes me swoon. Unfortunately, though, most BBQ sauces are *loaded* with refined white sugar and maybe even high fructose corn syrup. To add to the junk food train, regular pizza is usually made with refined flour, making it a high-carb, low-protein, and low-in-nutrients meal.

Instead, this clean pizza uses a whole wheat pita instead of pizza dough for an unrefined, higher protein, and higher fiber alternative. Plus, pita pizzas are way easier to make than regular pizza dough, take much less time, and are a breeze to clean up. The kicker on this pizza, though, is the clean BBQ sauce—it's *to die for* and full of so much flavor. Seriously: so much goodness piled onto your own individual pizza to enjoy!

FOR THE CLEAN BBQ SAUCE
1 tbsp (15 ml) olive oil
2 cloves garlic, minced
1 (8-oz [227-g]) can no-salt tomato sauce
2 tbsp (30 g) tomato paste
2 tbsp (40 g) molasses
2 tbsp (40 g) raw honey
1 tbsp (15 ml) apple cider vinegar
½ tsp granulated onion
¼ tsp sea salt
¼ tsp ground black pepper

FOR THE PIZZA
½ tsp sea salt
¼ tsp ground black pepper
¼ tsp paprika
⅛ tsp garlic powder
1 large boneless, skinless chicken breast
1 tbsp (15 ml) olive oil
4 whole wheat pita breads
3 oz (84 g) fresh mozzarella, sliced
¼ red onion, thinly sliced
¼ cup (4 g) chopped fresh cilantro, optional

Preheat the oven to 350°F (180°C), and line a baking sheet with parchment paper.

To make the BBQ sauce, heat the olive oil over medium-high heat in a saucepan, then add the garlic. Cook for 1 minute, until the garlic is fragrant, then add the tomato sauce, tomato paste, molasses, honey, vinegar, granulated onion, salt, and pepper, and stir to combine. Cook, stirring frequently, for 6 to 8 minutes, until the sauce is heated through and starting to thicken. Remove the sauce from the heat, and set it aside.

For the chicken, combine the salt, pepper, paprika, and garlic powder in a small mixing bowl, and stir well. Season the chicken breast liberally with this spice blend.

Heat the olive oil over medium-high heat in a large skillet. Add the chicken breast to the skillet, and cook for 4 to 6 minutes per side, until it's cooked through and browned on both sides. Then, remove the chicken from the heat, and slice it into small, bite-size pieces. Set aside.

To assemble the pizza, lay out the pita breads on the prepared baking sheet. (You may need to bake two pizzas at a time or use two baking sheets to avoid crowding the pizzas.) Spread approximately 2 tablespoons (30 ml) of the BBQ sauce over each of the pitas, leaving about ¼ inch (6 mm) around the edge for the crust. Refrigerate the remaining BBQ sauce in an airtight container for up to 5 days.

Arrange the chicken, mozzarella, and then the onion over the BBQ sauce on each pita.

Bake the pizzas for 6 to 8 minutes, until the edges of the crust become golden brown and the cheese is melted and bubbly. Remove the pizzas from the oven, slice into quarters, and top with the cilantro, if desired.

Note: These pizzas can be stored in the refrigerator for up to 4 days and are great reheated in the microwave or the oven.

QUINOA-CRUSTED CHICKEN STRIPS
with BUTTERNUT SQUASH MAC *and* CHEESE

Fortunately, this tasty recipe means you don't have to stay away from comfort foods. The chicken strips are baked, not fried, and coated with quinoa and chickpea flour instead of breadcrumbs. The mac and cheese eliminates refined carbs and fats by using whole wheat macaroni, butternut squash, almond milk, and a little bit of Parmesan. And to add fiber and vitamins, the combo is paired with a side of broccolini. So much yum!

FOR THE CHICKEN
2 cups (370 g) cooked quinoa
½ cup (60 g) almond flour
1 tsp sea salt
½ tsp garlic powder
½ tsp ground black pepper
2 eggs
½ cup (43 g) chickpea flour
1 lb (455 g) boneless, skinless chicken breasts, cut into strips

FOR THE MAC AND CHEESE
3 cups (315 g) whole wheat or quinoa elbow noodles
1 tbsp (15 ml) olive oil
½ yellow onion, diced
1 small butternut squash, peeled and diced
1½–2 cups (360–480 ml) low-sodium chicken broth, divided
¼ cup (60 ml) unsweetened almond milk
1 tsp sea salt
½ tsp garlic powder
⅓ cup (30 g) grated Parmesan cheese, plus more for garnish

FOR THE SAUTÉED BROCCOLINI
1 tbsp (15 ml) olive oil
1 lb (455 g) broccolini
1 shallot, minced
2 cloves garlic, minced
½ tsp sea salt
⅛ tsp crushed red pepper flakes
¼ cup (60 ml) low-sodium chicken broth

For the quinoa, preheat the oven to 350°F (180°C), and line a rimmed baking sheet with parchment.

Spread the quinoa on the prepared baking sheet, and bake it until it is toasted and golden brown, 20 to 22 minutes. Let cool, then add it to a shallow bowl, along with the almond flour, salt, garlic powder, and pepper. Stir to combine.

In a second shallow bowl, beat the eggs. In a third bowl, place the chickpea flour.

Increase the oven temperature to 475°F (240°C), and line a rimmed baking sheet with parchment paper.

Dredge the chicken strips into the chickpea flour, then the egg, then coat them with the quinoa crust. Place the coated chicken on the prepared baking sheet. Repeat until all the chicken has been used, arranging the pieces 2 inches (5 cm) apart. Do not crowd your pan; if necessary, use two baking sheets.

Bake the chicken for 8 to 10 minutes, then gently flip the pieces using kitchen tongs. Bake for 8 to 10 minutes more, then remove it from the oven.

To make the mac and cheese, heat a large pot of water over high heat, and bring it to a boil. Add the noodles and cook, stirring frequently, for 6 to 8 minutes, until the noodles are almost tender, but not fully cooked through. Drain the noodles, and set them aside in the pot used to cook them.

For the butternut squash sauce, heat the oil in a medium saucepan over medium-high heat. Add the onion, butternut squash, 1½ cups (360 ml) of the chicken broth, and the almond milk, and cook, stirring occasionally, until the onion and squash are tender, 10 to 15 minutes.

Transfer the squash mixture to a blender. Add the salt, garlic powder, and Parmesan, and puree until the mixture is completely smooth and creamy. This should yield about 4 cups (960 ml) of sauce. You can add some of the remaining ½ cup (120 ml) of chicken broth, if needed, to achieve a pourable, but not watery, consistency. Pour the sauce over the noodles and stir to combine. Top with additional Parmesan cheese, if desired.

To make the broccolini, in a large skillet over medium-high heat, heat the olive oil. Add the broccolini, shallot, garlic, salt, red pepper flakes, and chicken broth. Cover and cook until the broccolini is tender, 6 to 8 minutes.

TURKEY MEATLOAF, CAULIFLOWER MASH, *and* GARLIC PEAS

Meatloaf is the go-to comfort food during cold winter months. It's filling, it's hearty, and it's everything you crave and need when outside is cold and gloomy.

This meatloaf is made with lean turkey, cauliflower, and almond flour to reduce the percentage of fat and carbs without altering the taste too much. If you make it like this, you can include meatloaf in your diet on a regular basis, not only occasionally. You can also turn this meatloaf recipe into meatballs, just saying!

FOR THE MEATLOAF

1 lb (455 g) ground turkey
¾ cup (90 g) almond flour
2 tbsp (6 g) chopped fresh Italian parsley, plus more for garnish
½ cup (50 g) grated Parmesan cheese
1 tsp sea salt
½ tsp ground black pepper
¼ tsp garlic powder
1 egg
¾ cup (180 ml) warm water

FOR THE GLAZE

½ cup (120 ml) no-salt tomato sauce
1 tbsp (15 g) tomato paste
½ tbsp (10 g) raw honey
¼ tsp onion powder
½ tsp sea salt
½ tsp apple cider vinegar
⅛ tsp garlic powder
1½ tsp (5 g) coconut sugar
1½ tsp (3 g) dry mustard

FOR THE CAULIFLOWER MASH

1 tbsp (15 ml) olive oil
4 cups (340 g) riced cauliflower (see Note, page 39)
½ tsp sea salt
¼ tsp garlic powder
¾ cup (180 ml) unsweetened almond milk

FOR THE GARLIC PEAS

1 tbsp (15 ml) olive oil
2 cloves garlic, minced
2 cups (267 g) frozen peas, thawed
½ tsp sea salt
¼ tsp ground black pepper

For the meatloaf, preheat the oven to 325°F (160°C). In a large mixing bowl, combine the turkey, almond flour, parsley, Parmesan, salt, pepper, garlic powder, egg, and water.

Transfer the mixture to a 9 x 5–inch (23 x 12.5–cm) loaf pan.

To make the glaze, stir together the tomato sauce, tomato paste, honey, onion powder, salt, vinegar, garlic powder, coconut sugar, and mustard. Pour the glaze over the meatloaf, and spread it evenly.

Bake until the meatloaf reaches 160°F (70°C) on an instant-read thermometer, about 1 hour. Let it rest for 5 minutes before slicing.

Prepare the cauliflower mash while the meatloaf is in the oven. Heat a saucepan over medium-high heat, and add the olive oil. Add the cauliflower, salt, and garlic powder, and cook, stirring occasionally, for 3 to 4 minutes, or until the cauliflower begins to turn tender.

Add the milk to the pan, and bring it to a boil. Cover and cook until the cauliflower is fully tender, 10 to 12 minutes. Remove ½ cup (120 ml) of the liquid, and set it aside. Drain the remaining liquid from the cauliflower.

Mash the cauliflower using a potato masher, or puree using a food processor, adding some of the reserved liquid, as needed, to reach your desired consistency.

To make the garlic peas, in a skillet, heat the olive oil over medium-high heat. Add the garlic and cook, stirring frequently, until golden, about 1 to 2 minutes, then add the peas. Season with the salt and pepper, and cook until heated through, about 2 minutes. Garnish with parsley, if desired.

Exciting and Vibrant
SALADS

In order to live a clean lifestyle, we have to eat tons of veggies. Well, at least, it's a really good idea, because veggies are rich in vitamins and minerals, and they increase the level of antioxidants in our bodies, which is always a great thing.

What better way to eat veggies than to combine them in a salad, right? It's probably the easiest and most convenient way. Plus, making a salad takes so little time, compared to foods that require more cooking and baking. Salads are so versatile, and you can combine many flavors, textures, and colors, which makes them definitely not boring. If you ever thought they were, you'll change your mind after you read this chapter.

Not all salads are created equal. Some salads are definitely not good for you. The most common culprit that ruins an otherwise healthy salad is the dressing that, more often than not, is loaded with saturated fat, sugar, and sodium.

The good news is you can easily make a well-balanced, satisfying, and fun salad. All you have to do is to make your own salad and replace the unhealthy ingredients with clean, whole, nutritious ingredients. Kick up your regular 7-layer taco dip (page 125), and make it in salad form. Enjoy all the colors of the rainbow in the Rainbow Detox Salad with Sesame-Ginger Peanut Dressing (page 130), and feel full and satisfied with Your New Go-To Pasta Salad (page 137), which is insanely flavorful, creamy, and delicious.

Are you excited to try all the vibrant colors, flavors, and textures?

This chapter will change your perception of salads for good. It will show you that it's easy to make a fun, delicious salad that is packed with minerals, vitamins, and proteins without compromising on taste.

7-LAYER TACO SALAD

Ditch the tortilla and make a 7-Layer Taco Salad. This salad is a great way to satisfy your taco cravings and to incorporate ingredients that are good for you into your diet. I made this salad vegetarian, but it's still rich in protein from the quinoa and the Greek yogurt I used in the dressing. Quinoa is rich in protein and fiber, and contains minerals—including calcium, magnesium, phosphorus, iron, and potassium— antioxidants, and vitamins E and B. Quinoa is a nutritional powerhouse.

This taco salad also contains good fats from the avocado. It's satisfying, filling, and nutritious at the same time. And don't even get me started on the incredible taste and wonderful flavors. This 7-Layer Taco Salad is a bowl of fresh, hearty goodness you can prep ahead and enjoy for lunch or dinner. Feel free to add in meat if you'd like!

FOR THE SALAD

1 tbsp (15 ml) olive oil

2 cups (310 g) fresh or frozen corn kernels

½ tsp chili powder

½ tsp sea salt

¼ tsp ground black pepper

¼ tsp paprika

2 cups (370 g) cooked quinoa

3 cups (140 g) romaine lettuce, chopped

2 (15-oz [425-g]) cans black beans with no salt added, drained and rinsed

1 cup (160 g) grape tomatoes, halved

2 (2.25-oz [64-g]) cans sliced black olives, drained

2 avocados, diced

FOR THE TACO RANCH DRESSING

½ cup (120 g) plain full-fat Greek yogurt

¼ cup (60 ml) unsweetened almond milk

1 tbsp (15 ml) freshly squeezed lime juice

¼ tsp dried dill

¼ tsp garlic powder

1 tsp onion powder

¼ tsp coconut sugar

¼ tsp sea salt

½ tsp ground cumin

¼ tsp ground black pepper

½ tsp paprika

¼ tsp dried oregano

⅛ tsp cayenne pepper

To make the salad, heat the oil in a large nonstick skillet over medium-high heat. Add the corn, chili powder, salt, pepper, and paprika, and cook for 8 to 10 minutes, or until the corn starts to brown, stirring occasionally. Set aside the corn to cool.

In a deep, clear glass bowl, place the quinoa, followed by a layer of the lettuce, then the black beans, then the pan-roasted corn, then the tomatoes, then the olives and the avocados. For each layer, begin by placing the food around the perimeter of the bowl to define the layer, and then fill the middle with the rest.

For the dressing, whisk together well in a medium bowl the yogurt, milk, lime juice, dill, garlic powder, onion powder, coconut sugar, salt, cumin, black pepper, paprika, oregano, and cayenne.

Drizzle the dressing over the salad.

Alternatively, you could stack this salad in a 1-quart (1-L) Mason jar, starting with the salad dressing, then the tomatoes, black beans, corn, olives, quinoa, avocado, and finally add the lettuce to the very top. When you are ready to eat the salad, pour it into a large mixing bowl, and toss to coat with the dressing.

CHIPOTLE CHICKEN SALAD *with* CILANTRO-LIME RANCH DRESSING

While you can use chipotle chicken in many dishes such as burritos, tacos, and enchiladas, I really like it in a salad paired with mixed baby greens, cilantro, grape tomatoes, avocado, and black beans and drizzled with ranch dressing. Unfortunately, ranch dressing is often made with mayonnaise, sour cream, and even sugar—ingredients that are neither nutritious nor low in calories. But you can make a homemade ranch with Greek yogurt, lime juice, cilantro, seasonings, and spices that will make you forget about the store-bought ranch forever. This is a flavorful and filling salad that's both good for you and delicious.

FOR THE CHIPOTLE CHICKEN

1 lb (455 g) boneless, skinless chicken breasts

½ tsp sea salt

½ tsp ground black pepper

¼ cup plus 1 tbsp (75 ml) olive oil, divided

1 canned chipotle pepper in adobo sauce, minced

1 tbsp (20 g) raw honey

1 tbsp (15 g) Dijon mustard

2 tbsp (2 g) chopped fresh cilantro

2 cloves garlic, minced

FOR THE CILANTRO-LIME RANCH DRESSING

1 cup (240 g) plain full-fat Greek yogurt

2 tbsp (30 ml) freshly squeezed lime juice

1 tbsp (15 ml) olive oil

⅓ cup (80 ml) unsweetened almond milk

⅓ cup (5 g) chopped fresh cilantro

¼ tsp dried dill

2 tbsp (6 g) roughly chopped fresh chives

2 cloves garlic, minced

½ tsp sea salt

¼ tsp ground black pepper

FOR THE SALAD

6 cups (200 g) mixed baby greens

1 cup (160 g) grape tomatoes, halved

¼ cup (4 g) chopped fresh cilantro

4 green onions, sliced

1 avocado, sliced

½ cup (130 g) black beans

For the chicken, place in a large resealable bag or refrigerator-safe storage container the chicken, salt, black pepper, ¼ cup (60 ml) of the olive oil, chipotle pepper, honey, mustard, cilantro, and garlic. Press the chicken around to fully coat it. Seal the bag tightly to ensure no leakage, and then marinate the chicken in the refrigerator for at least 30 minutes, or up to 8 hours.

To make the cilantro-lime ranch dressing, place the yogurt, lime juice, olive oil, milk, cilantro, dill, chives, garlic, salt, and pepper in a blender or food processor, and blend until smooth and creamy.

Once the chicken has marinated, heat the remaining 1 tablespoon (15 ml) of the olive oil in a large skillet over medium-high heat. Add the chicken, and cook it for 4 to 6 minutes per side, until it's cooked through and brown on both sides. Then, remove the chicken from the heat, slice it, and set it aside.

To make the salad, layer the greens in a large bowl, followed by the sliced chicken, tomatoes, cilantro, green onions, avocado, and black beans.

Drizzle with the salad dressing and serve.

KALE *and* QUINOA MEDITERRANEAN SALAD

Leafy greens make the best salads. They are packed with fiber, nutrients, vitamins, and minerals. Especially during the fall and winter seasons, kale is my go-to leafy green. For this salad, I chose to combine kale with quinoa—a great source of protein—in a fresh, vibrant salad served with a homemade Greek dressing.

To make the salad extra special, I decided to give it a wonderful Mediterranean twist by adding in cherry tomatoes, fresh cucumber, Kalamata olives, red onion, chickpeas, and feta cheese. This salad makes a deliciously light lunch or dinner. Suddenly kale salad is starting to sound interesting, am I right?

FOR THE SALAD

1 cup (180 g) quinoa
2 cups (480 ml) water
3 cups (200 g) chopped kale
1 tsp olive oil
1 cup (150 g) cherry tomatoes, halved
1 cup (120 g) peeled and diced cucumber
⅓ cup (50 g) finely diced red onion
¾ cup (130 g) Kalamata olives, halved
1 (15-oz [425-g]) can chickpeas, with no salt added, drained and rinsed
¼ cup (38) crumbled feta, plus more for garnish

FOR THE GREEK DRESSING

¼ cup (60 ml) olive oil
1 tbsp (15 ml) red wine vinegar
1 tbsp (15 g) Dijon mustard
2 tsp (10 ml) freshly squeezed lemon juice
¼ tsp dried oregano
1 clove garlic, minced
1 tsp raw honey
¼ tsp sea salt

For the salad, rinse the quinoa in a fine-mesh sieve to remove any debris and dirt. In a medium saucepan, cook the quinoa over medium-high heat for 6 to 8 minutes, tossing frequently, to toast the quinoa. It's done when the quinoa is no longer wet and begins to pop and turn golden brown. Add the water to the pan, bring it to a boil, and then reduce the heat to a simmer. Cook, covered, until all of the liquid is absorbed and the quinoa has doubled in size, 15 to 20 minutes. Then, fluff the quinoa with a fork, and allow it to cool.

Add the kale to a large mixing bowl, and drizzle it with the olive oil. Using your hands, massage the kale with the olive oil for 2 to 3 minutes to soften the kale.

Add the tomatoes, cucumber, onion, olives, chickpeas, feta, and 1½ cups (275 g) of the cooked quinoa, and toss well.

To make the Greek dressing, in a small bowl, combine the olive oil, red wine vinegar, mustard, lemon juice, oregano, garlic, honey, and salt, and whisk together vigorously until emulsified. Drizzle the dressing over the salad, and toss once more to coat.

Garnish the salad with feta cheese, and serve immediately.

Note: If you store this salad for later use during the week, add the dressing just before serving to avoid any soggy ingredients.

RAINBOW DETOX SALAD *with* SESAME-GINGER PEANUT DRESSING

I call this a detox salad because it is great for cleansing the body to help it eliminate toxins. Detox salads are helpful after the holidays, when most people indulge in dishes and desserts that contain added sugar and fats, and tons of carbs. They are also perfect after cheat days, for those of us who follow a clean lifestyle with little exceptions here and there.

Detox salads can be fun, colorful, refreshing, and filled with tasty ingredients. Add all the colors of the rainbow in the form of whole ingredients, and you get vibrant salad. This one is made with kale, carrots, cilantro, red cabbage, almonds, yellow bell pepper, green onions, and edamame. Can you picture all these amazing colors together? What about the amazing flavors? Rainbow goodness! To add even more amazing flavors, you have a homemade sesame-ginger peanut dressing that brings the salad together.

FOR THE SESAME-GINGER PEANUT DRESSING

1 tbsp (15 ml) toasted sesame oil
2 tbsp (30 g) natural peanut butter
2 tsp (14 g) raw honey
1 tbsp (15 ml) low-sodium soy sauce
2 tsp (10 ml) freshly squeezed lime juice
½ tsp crushed red pepper flakes
1 tsp minced ginger
Hot water

FOR THE SALAD

2 cups (135 g) finely chopped kale leaves
2 cups (180 g) finely chopped red cabbage
1 cup (110 g) shredded carrots
¾ cup (12 g) roughly chopped fresh cilantro
½ yellow bell pepper, thinly sliced
⅓ cup (35 g) toasted, slivered raw almonds
⅓ cup (16 g) thinly sliced green onions
1 cup (150 g) frozen shelled edamame, thawed

Prepare the dressing by adding the sesame oil, peanut butter, honey, soy sauce, lime juice, crushed red pepper flakes, and ginger to a blender. Blend on high until fully pureed. If the dressing is too thick, add 1 tablespoon (15 ml) of hot water at a time and blend again, until the dressing is thin enough to toss with the salad.

To make the salad, add the kale, red cabbage, carrots, cilantro, bell pepper, almonds, green onions, and edamame to a large bowl, and toss to combine.

To serve, drizzle the salad with the dressing, and toss the salad to coat.

THAI STEAK SALAD *with* SPICY PEANUT BUTTER DRESSING

This salad is anything but boring or bland: it's a mix of salty, spicy, sour, and sweet. Gotta love all those toppings, too!

Making a Thai Steak Salad involves prepping the three salad components: the dressing, the steak, and the salad. The steak is a thin slice of beef seasoned perfectly with salt and pepper. The salad is a mix of fresh veggies and herbs, plus peanuts for extra texture. The dressing is a flavorful Thai classic made with soy sauce, peanut butter, lime juice, ginger, coconut sugar, jalapeño, and chili flakes. All these wonderful flavors are combined in a totally delicious salad that is quick and easy to make.

FOR THE SPICY PEANUT BUTTER DRESSING

2 tbsp (30 ml) low-sodium soy sauce

½ jalapeño pepper, seeded and chopped

1 tbsp (15 g) natural peanut butter

1 tsp lime zest

1 tbsp (15 ml) freshly squeezed lime juice

1 clove garlic

½" (12-mm) piece ginger

1 tsp coconut sugar

¼ tsp crushed red pepper flakes

Hot water

FOR THE STEAK

½ tbsp (8 ml) olive oil

1 lb (455 g) 1" (2.5-cm)-thick New York strip steak

½ tsp sea salt

¼ tsp ground black pepper

FOR THE SALAD

2 cups (70 g) mixed baby greens

1 cup (160 g) grape tomatoes, halved

1 cucumber, halved lengthwise and cut into half-moon slices

¼ cup (40 g) red onion, thinly sliced

¼ cup (23 g) loosely packed fresh mint leaves

3 tbsp (3 g) chopped fresh cilantro

2 tbsp (20 g) chopped peanuts

To make the dressing, add the soy sauce, jalapeño, peanut butter, lime zest and juice, garlic, ginger, coconut sugar, and crushed red pepper flakes to a blender. Blend until smooth. If the dressing is too thick, add hot water, 1 tablespoon (15 ml) at a time, and blend the dressing again until it's thin enough to toss with the salad. Set aside the dressing.

For the steak, heat the oil in a skillet over medium-high heat. Season the steak with the salt and pepper. Sear the steak until it is browned well on one side, 5 to 6 minutes. Flip the steak over, and cook until the second side is dark brown and the meat is medium rare, 5 to 6 more minutes. Transfer the steak to a cutting board and let it rest for 5 minutes. Slice the steak thinly, across the grain.

To serve, place the mixed baby greens in a bowl, then arrange the sliced steak, tomatoes, cucumber, onion, mint, and cilantro on top. Drizzle the salad with the dressing, and top with the peanuts.

The ULTIMATE CHOPPED ITALIAN SALAD

Chopped Italian salad proves that simple recipes made with fresh ingredients are the best recipes. This salad is loaded with ingredients that complement each other wonderfully and create a deliciously amazing mix of flavors, textures, and colors.

We have greens, artichoke hearts, beans, cucumber, grape tomatoes, three types of olives, red onion, the mandatory pepperoncini, uncured salami, and Parmesan cheese. All these ingredients are then mixed with a lovely Italian dressing to create the ultimate chopped salad.

This salad will disappear from your plate in a matter of minutes, which is a great thing, because it's good for you.

FOR THE ITALIAN DRESSING
½ cup (120 ml) olive oil
⅓ cup (30 g) grated Parmesan cheese
¼ cup (60 ml) red wine vinegar
1 tbsp (15 g) Dijon mustard
1 tsp onion powder
1 tsp garlic powder
1 tsp sea salt
1 tsp dried oregano
1 tsp ground black pepper

FOR THE SALAD
4 cups (140 g) mixed baby greens, ideally to include baby romaine and radicchio
1 (15-oz [425-g]) can artichoke hearts, drained and quartered
1 (15-oz [425-g]) can chickpeas with no salt added, drained and rinsed
½ large cucumber, diced
1 cup (160 g) grape tomatoes, halved
½ cup (90 g) green olives
½ cup (90 g) black olives
¼ cup (45 g) Kalamata olives
½ small red onion, thinly sliced
6 pepperoncini, thinly sliced
4 oz (113 g) thinly sliced uncured salami
2 oz (57 g) Parmesan cheese, shaved

To make the dressing, place the olive oil, Parmesan, vinegar, mustard, onion powder, garlic powder, salt, oregano, and pepper in a mixing bowl or jar, and whisk to combine thoroughly. Set aside the dressing while you prepare the salad.

For the salad, place the greens, artichokes, chickpeas, cucumber, tomatoes, green, black, and Kalamata olives, onion, pepperoncini, salami, and Parmesan in a large mixing bowl. Toss the salad to combine the ingredients. Drizzle it with the salad dressing, and toss once again to coat evenly.

Note: If prepping this recipe for later use, add the dressing just before you eat the salad so the lettuce and softer veggies don't get soggy.

YOUR NEW GO-TO PASTA SALAD

Despite their unhealthy reputation, pasta salads don't have to be bad for you. There are actually a ton of fun and tasty ways to make them clean: replacing store-bought dressing with a homemade dressing, substituting processed meats with lean proteins, and loading them with fresh veggies.

So far so good, right? To make things easier, I present to you—Your New Go-To Pasta Salad, a fresh and tasty pasta salad made with a creamy and absolutely delicious avocado dressing that's made with only real ingredients. Plus, I have added chickpeas, arugula, and whole-grain pasta for added fiber, protein, and nutrients. That avocado dressing is so creamy, you'll think you're cheating!

FOR THE SALAD

2 cups (300 g) cherry tomatoes, halved

1 tsp olive oil, plus more for the pasta, optional

½ tsp sea salt

½ tsp ground black pepper

1 lb (455 g) whole wheat, super-grain, or chickpea penne pasta

1 cup (20 g) baby arugula, packed

1 (15-oz [425-g]) can chickpeas with no salt added, drained and rinsed

2 tbsp (15 g) crumbled feta, plus more for garnish

FOR THE CREAMY AVOCADO DRESSING

1 cup (30 g) loosely packed fresh baby spinach

2 avocados

Freshly squeezed juice of 1 large lemon

1 clove garlic

½ tsp sea salt

¼ tsp ground black pepper

For the salad, preheat the oven to 400°F (200°C), and line a rimmed baking sheet with parchment paper.

Add the tomatoes to the baking sheet, followed by the olive oil, salt, and pepper. Toss to coat. Roast the tomatoes for 15 to 20 minutes, until the tomatoes are soft and the skins begin to shrivel. Remove the pan from the oven, and set it aside to let the tomatoes cool.

Bring a large pot of water to a boil over high heat. Once boiling, add the pasta and cook it according to the package instructions, then drain and set it aside. You can drizzle the pasta with olive oil and toss it to prevent sticking, if desired.

For the dressing, in a food processor or blender, combine the spinach, avocados, lemon juice, garlic, salt, and pepper. Pulse until the dressing is creamy and smooth.

To assemble the salad, arrange the cooked pasta, arugula, chickpeas, feta, and roasted tomatoes in a large mixing bowl, and top with the dressing and feta crumbles.

Note: Your New Go-To Pasta Salad can be served hot or cold and makes a great, filling meal-prep lunch.

Lunch Bowls
OF GOODNESS

Dinner seems to be the meal of the day where people look for new recipes to try, meaning lunch is usually an afterthought. For lunch, more often than not, people eat out or get fast food. We already know those are not always the healthiest or most nutritious options, nor the most fun.

When you decide to make lunch at home and pack it for work, it can be easy to resort to sandwiches, because they are simple and easy to make. While, as I hope to show you in this cookbook, sandwiches and salads can be amazing lunch options, a little variation is the key to success, and lunch bowls are a fantastic and easy way to up your lunch game.

While you may not have a lot of time to prep three meals from scratch every day, especially meals that take a lot of time to cook, I still believe variation is possible. I don't have a lot of time on my hands, either, so please trust me on this one—I really get you if you're skeptical.

Sometimes, making lunch from scratch requires only the right combination of ingredients and a big bowl or an airtight container with a lid, if you want to take the lunch with you to the office. How is that possible?

Lunch bowls!

The formula for lunch bowls is very simple: mix protein with veggies and whole grains. You can even use leftovers from dinner, if you don't have time to cook protein or veggies from scratch.

To make lunch bowls even easier for you, in this chapter I will give you all the tips you need to make the prepping of these fantastic lunches easy and fun. Plus, recipes, of course. By the end of this chapter, you'll be fascinated by the endless possibilities.

BBQ PULLED CHICKEN BOWL *with* ROASTED CARROTS *and* CABBAGE SLAW

BBQ chicken is for . . . BBQs, right? Well, yes, of course. But who says you cannot enjoy it for lunch as well? Pair it with sweet and yummy roasted carrots and crunchy cabbage slaw, and your lunch planning is done. This bowl gives you perfection in taste and texture.

FOR THE ROASTED CARROTS

10 large carrots, peeled and sliced diagonally into bite-size pieces
1 tbsp (15 ml) olive oil
¼ tsp sea salt
¼ tsp ground black pepper

FOR THE BBQ PULLED CHICKEN

½ tbsp (8 ml) olive oil
½ lb (230 g) boneless, skinless chicken breasts
½ lb (230 g) boneless, skinless chicken thighs
½ cup (120 ml) no-salt tomato sauce
½ tsp garlic powder
¼ tsp granulated onion
1 tbsp (15 g) tomato paste
1 tbsp (20 g) molasses
1 tbsp (20 g) raw honey
½ tbsp (8 ml) apple cider vinegar
⅛ tsp sea salt
⅛ tsp ground black pepper

FOR THE CABBAGE SLAW

2 tbsp (30 g) plain full-fat Greek yogurt
1 tbsp (15 ml) extra virgin olive oil
2 tbsp (30 ml) apple cider vinegar
¼ tsp sea salt
¼ tsp ground black pepper, to taste
½ small head green cabbage, shredded
⅓ small head red cabbage, shredded
¼ small red onion, sliced thin

FOR SERVING

Black sesame seeds
2 green onions, sliced

For the carrots, preheat the oven to 400°F (200°C), and line a large rimmed baking sheet with parchment paper. Place the carrots on the baking sheet, then drizzle with the olive oil, salt, and pepper. Toss until the carrots are coated, and then arrange them in a single layer. Roast the carrots until they have caramelized on the edges and are easily pierced through with a fork, 20 to 30 minutes. Toss the carrots halfway through the cooking time, so they cook evenly. Set aside the carrots.

To make the BBQ pulled chicken, heat the olive oil over medium-high heat in a large skillet. Add the chicken breasts and thighs, tomato sauce, garlic powder, granulated onion, tomato paste, molasses, honey, vinegar, salt, and pepper. Toss to coat the chicken. Cover and cook, flipping the chicken occasionally, for 12 to 16 minutes, or until the chicken is cooked through and tender. Remove the chicken using tongs or a slotted spoon, and set it on a cutting board or large plate. Using two forks, pull the chicken apart into bite-size pieces that resemble shredded chicken.

While shredding the chicken, heat the BBQ sauce remaining in the pan over medium-high heat until it's reduced by one-third. Then, toss the pulled chicken with the sauce.

To make the slaw, in a large bowl, whisk the yogurt, olive oil, vinegar, salt, and pepper until it's combined well. Add the green and red cabbage and onion, and toss to coat with the dressing.

To assemble the meal, in each of four bowls arrange one-quarter of the slaw, the roasted carrots, and the pulled chicken. Top the slaw with the black sesame seeds and the entire bowl with the sliced green onions.

 Note: If you make this recipe ahead for meal prep for the week, store the coleslaw separately from the carrots and pulled chicken, then add it to the bowl after the carrots and chicken are reheated. This will keep the coleslaw crunchy and cold.

CHICKEN CAPRESE BOWL

Caprese salad—the simple yet wonderful Italian salad made with mozzarella, tomatoes, and fresh basil—is a great appetizer. The salad is nutritious, and it has simple flavors that go together wonderfully. But it's not filling enough to eat it for lunch on its own. However, when you combine it with chicken and other veggies, you've got yourself a filling lunch.

The Chicken Caprese Bowl is made with chicken breast, spiralized zucchini, balsamic vinaigrette, and the staple caprese salad ingredients—mozzarella, cherry tomatoes, and fresh basil leaves. So simple, yet so tasty and satisfying.

FOR THE BALSAMIC VINAIGRETTE

3 tbsp (45 ml) balsamic vinegar

2 tbsp (30 ml) olive oil

½ tsp sea salt

¼ tsp ground black pepper

FOR THE CHICKEN

1 tbsp (15 ml) olive oil

1½ lb (685 g) boneless, skinless chicken breasts

½ tsp sea salt

¼ tsp ground black pepper

⅛ tsp garlic powder

FOR THE BOWL

4 medium zucchini, spiralized

1 cup (112 g) diced fresh mozzarella

2 cups (300 g) cherry tomatoes, halved

8 basil leaves, for garnish

For the vinaigrette, in a small mixing bowl, combine the balsamic vinegar, olive oil, salt, and pepper. Use a whisk or a fork to bring the ingredients together until the dressing is emulsified.

For the chicken, heat the olive oil over medium-high heat in a large skillet. Season the chicken with the salt, pepper, and garlic powder. Cook the chicken in the pan for 4 to 6 minutes on each side, until golden brown and cooked through. Then, remove the chicken from the heat, leaving behind any remaining oil. Allow the chicken to rest for 5 minutes, then slice it, and set it aside.

For the bowl, add the zucchini to the pan you used to cook the chicken. Cook the zucchini over medium-high heat for 2 to 3 minutes, until it's tender, but not mushy.

In a medium bowl, combine the mozzarella and tomatoes. Slice the basil leaves.

To assemble the bowls, start with a layer of the zucchini, topped with the sliced chicken and then the cheese-tomato mixture. Drizzle the balsamic vinaigrette over the top and garnish with the basil.

SHEET-PAN HAWAIIAN KEBABS *and* TURMERIC-COCONUT RICE BOWL

I don't know about you, but Hawaiian kebabs give me major joy. Probably because they are perfect for summer BBQs, when everybody's stress levels are lower. The same thing goes for turmeric-coconut rice—try to be in a bad mood while you enjoy that creamy goodness, I dare you! This lunch bowl combines the amazing flavors of these two summer dishes in a lighter and healthier version. Plus, using a sheet pan makes this process so much easier, with a quick cleanup. The killer teriyaki sauce is like the cherry on top.

FOR THE TURMERIC-COCONUT RICE
2½ cups (600 ml) low-sodium chicken broth

1 (13.5-oz [400-ml]) can full-fat coconut milk, shaken

1 tsp ground turmeric

¾ tsp sea salt

2 cups (370 g) brown rice

FOR THE TERIYAKI SAUCE
½ cup (120 ml) low-sodium soy sauce

¼ cup (85 g) raw honey

2 cloves garlic, minced

1 tsp minced ginger

1½ tsp (8 ml) freshly squeezed lime juice

¼ tsp crushed red pepper flakes

1 tsp arrowroot starch

¾ cup (180 ml) water

FOR THE TERIYAKI CHICKEN SKEWERS
1 lb (455 g) boneless, skinless chicken thighs, cut into cubes

2 medium zucchini, sliced thick

1 large red bell pepper, sliced into large strips

1 pineapple, cut into cubes

1 large red onion, sliced thick

4 skewers (if using wood skewers, make sure to soak in water for at least 15 minutes)

1 tsp sesame seeds

To make the rice, combine the chicken broth, coconut milk, turmeric, salt, and rice in a deep stockpot, and heat it over medium-high heat. Bring to a simmer and cook, covered, for 25 minutes, or until the liquid is fully absorbed and the rice is creamy, stirring occasionally.

To make the teriyaki sauce, heat the soy sauce, honey, garlic, ginger, lime juice, and crushed red pepper flakes in a medium saucepan over medium-high heat. Simmer for 4 to 6 minutes to cook the garlic.

In a small bowl, combine the arrowroot starch and water until mixed well. Add this mixture to the teriyaki sauce, and stir to combine. Cook, stirring occasionally, for 3 to 5 minutes, or until the sauce thickens. Remove the sauce from the heat, and let it cool for 5 to 8 minutes.

For the skewers, thread the chicken, zucchini, bell pepper, pineapple, and red onion onto the skewers, repeating until the skewers are full. Place the skewers on a baking pan.

When the teriyaki sauce is cooled, pour ½ cup (120 ml) over the skewers and allow them to marinate for at least 20 minutes or, refrigerated, for up to 8 hours.

While the skewers are marinating, put a rack in the center of the oven and preheat it to 450°F (230°C).

Bake the skewers on the center rack of the oven for 10 minutes, turning over once. Then, bake for 10 to 15 minutes longer, until the vegetables are tender and the chicken is cooked through.

To serve, lay out the skewers over the coconut rice, then drizzle them with the remaining teriyaki sauce. Sprinkle with the sesame seeds.

 Note: Make this recipe ahead of time for a great meal-prep lunch bowl.

MEDITERRANEAN CHICKEN *and* QUINOA BOWL *with* CUCUMBER DRESSING

I'm a huge fan of Mediterranean food because the key ingredients are fresh veggies, leafy greens, legumes, whole grains, and lean proteins, such as seafood and chicken. This makes it an easy cuisine to enjoy as part of a clean, unrefined-food lifestyle. This recipe embraces the authenticity of Mediterranean cuisine and brings you a bowl of goodness that will make you excited about your lunch break. It's filled with fresh, clean ingredients, including romaine lettuce, cucumber, grape tomatoes, red onion, Kalamata olives, and feta cheese, stacked over a quinoa base, topped with chicken breast, and drizzled with a homemade cucumber dressing. Excuse me while I drool!

FOR THE MEDITERRANEAN CHICKEN AND QUINOA BOWL

1 tbsp (15 ml) olive oil

1 lb (455 g) boneless, skinless chicken breasts

½ tsp sea salt

½ tsp ground black pepper

2 cups (370 g) cooked quinoa

4 cups (190 g) roughly chopped romaine lettuce leaves

1 large cucumber, sliced into half moons

1 cup (160 g) grape tomatoes, halved

½ red onion, sliced

1 avocado, diced

⅓ cup (60 g) sliced Kalamata olives

½ cup (75 g) crumbled feta cheese

CUCUMBER DRESSING

½ cup (120 g) plain full-fat Greek yogurt

1 cup (133 g) peeled and diced cucumber

1 tbsp (15 g) tahini

1 tbsp (10 g) hemp seed hearts

2 tbsp (30 ml) unsweetened almond milk

1 clove garlic

¼ tsp sea salt

¼ tsp ground black pepper

2 tbsp (30 ml) freshly squeezed lemon juice

1 tsp chopped fresh dill

For the chicken, heat the olive oil over medium-high heat in a skillet. Season the chicken on both sides with the salt and pepper. Add the chicken to the hot oil, and cook until it is golden brown on both sides and cooked through, 4 to 6 minutes per side. Then, remove it from the heat, and allow it to rest for 5 minutes. Cut it into bite-size slices and set aside.

For the dressing, in a food processor or blender, combine the yogurt, cucumber, tahini, hemp seed hearts, almond milk, garlic, salt, pepper, lemon juice, and dill. Blend until smooth.

To prepare the bowl, make a base of quinoa at the bottom of the bowl. In small piles on top of the quinoa, arrange the chicken, lettuce, cucumber, tomatoes, onion, avocado, olives, and feta cheese. Drizzle with the dressing and serve.

MISO-GLAZED SALMON, SESAME SOBA NOODLES, and BOK CHOY

Anything with salmon will likely make me swoon, but I am especially in love with this miso-glazed salmon, because it is paired with whole-grain soba noodles and savory bok choy. By making this lunch at home, you'll avoid unnecessary fat, carbs, excess sodium, and all the processed ingredients you'd get at a restaurant, all while having full control of the taste and flavor of the dish. This is the perfect lunch bowl made with clean ingredients, and is deceptively easy to make, too!

FOR THE SALMON

3 tbsp (51 g) white miso paste

2 tbsp (30 ml) low-sodium soy sauce

2 tbsp (30 ml) rice vinegar

½ tbsp (4 g) minced ginger

1 tbsp (20 g) raw honey

1 tbsp (15 ml) sesame oil

2 cloves garlic, minced

4 (4-oz [113-g]) salmon fillets, skinned

FOR THE BOK CHOY

4 baby bok choy, quartered

FOR THE SOBA NOODLES

8 oz (226 g) dried whole-grain soba noodles

2 tsp (10 ml) sesame oil

2 tsp (10 ml) low-sodium soy sauce

¼ tsp sesame seeds

FOR THE QUICK CARROT SALAD

1 large carrot, sliced into matchsticks

2 tsp (10 ml) rice vinegar

½ tsp sesame seeds

FOR SERVING

2 green onions, sliced

1 tsp sesame seeds

For the salmon, in a small bowl, combine the miso paste, soy sauce, rice vinegar, ginger, honey, sesame oil, and garlic. Place the salmon in a glass baking dish and pour three-fourths of the marinade over the salmon. Marinate the salmon for 30 minutes in the refrigerator. Keep the reserved marinade for the bok choy.

While the salmon is marinating, preheat the oven to 350°F (180°C), and line a rimmed baking sheet with parchment paper.

Arrange the salmon on the baking sheet and surround it with the bok choy. Drizzle the reserved marinade over the bok choy. Bake the fish and bok choy for 20 minutes, until the salmon is flaky when twisted with a fork. To add a delicious crispy crust to the tops, preheat the broiler to high. Return the pan to the oven, and broil the fish for 1 minute, but watch carefully.

Prepare the noodles while the salmon and the bok choy are in the oven. Bring a large pot of water to a rapid boil. Add the soba, and use tongs to spread out the noodles. Cook for 2½ minutes. Then, immediately drain the soba noodles, rinse them with cold water, and transfer them to a medium bowl. Toss the cooled soba with the sesame oil, soy sauce, and sesame seeds.

For the carrot salad, in a separate small bowl, combine the carrot, rice vinegar, and sesame seeds. Toss to coat the carrots, then set aside.

For serving, make a base in a bowl with the soba noodles. Arrange the salmon, bok choy, and carrot salad on top of the noodles. Sprinkle with the green onions and sesame seeds.

 Note: This sheet-pan meal is a great quick lunch to make. If you prepare it ahead, store the cooked soba and carrot salad separately, and add them to the bowl after you reheat the salmon and bok choy.

SHRIMP FAJITAS *with* SMASHED CITRUS BLACK BEANS *and* MEXICAN RICE

Fajitas are one of my favorite lunches, because you can combine so many wonderful flavors—such as the fajita bell peppers and onions, the creamy and spicy beans, and the Mexican rice—and top them all off with tart lime juice and fresh cilantro. With this fajita bowl, you get all those delicious and complementary flavors and tastes, but the unhealthy ingredients have been ditched for unrefined options.

FOR THE MEXICAN RICE

2–3 medium tomatoes, divided

½ small yellow onion, quartered

2 cloves garlic

1 tbsp (15 ml) olive oil

1½ cups (280 g) long-grain brown rice

1 large jalapeño pepper, seeded and finely chopped

3 cups (720 ml) vegetable broth

2 tbsp (30 g) tomato paste

1 tsp sea salt

½ tsp ground cumin

¼ tsp paprika

½ cup (8 g) finely chopped fresh cilantro, plus more for serving

FOR THE FAJITA VEGGIES

1 tbsp (15 ml) olive oil

1 white onion, sliced

1 poblano chile, sliced

2 red bell peppers, sliced

1 green bell pepper, sliced

1 tsp sea salt

½ tsp ground black pepper

1 tsp ground cumin

To make the rice, in a food processor or blender, combine 2 of the tomatoes, the onion, and garlic, and process until smooth. This should yield 2 cups (480 ml). If it does not, add the remaining tomato, and process the mixture again, until smooth.

Heat the olive oil in a large saucepan over medium-high heat. Add the rice and jalapeño and cook, stirring occasionally, for 2 to 3 minutes. Add the tomato mixture, vegetable broth, tomato paste, salt, cumin, and paprika. Bring the mixture to a boil, then reduce it to a simmer. Cover the pan and cook until the liquid is absorbed and the rice is tender, 20 to 25 minutes, stirring occasionally. Stir in the cilantro, and set aside the rice.

To make the fajita veggies, in a large skillet, heat the olive oil over medium-high heat. Add the onion, poblano, red and green bell peppers, salt, pepper, and cumin, and toss to combine. Cook over medium-high heat until the bell peppers and onion are tender, 4 to 6 minutes.

(CONTINUED)

FOR THE SMASHED CITRUS BLACK BEANS

1 tbsp (15 ml) olive oil

1 clove garlic, minced

1 jalapeño pepper, seeded and minced

1 (15-oz [425-g]) can black beans with no salt added, drained and rinsed

¼ cup (60 ml) vegetable broth

½ tsp ground cumin

½ tsp chili powder

½ tsp paprika

½ tsp sea salt

2 tbsp (30 ml) freshly squeezed lime juice

½ tsp lime zest

FOR THE SHRIMP

1 tbsp (15 ml) olive oil

1 lb (455 g) large, raw deveined shrimp

1 tsp garlic powder

½ tsp chili powder

¼ tsp cayenne pepper

¼ tsp ground black pepper

1 tsp sea salt

FOR SERVING

Lime wedges

To make the beans, heat the olive oil over medium-high heat in a skillet. Once hot, add the garlic and jalapeño, and cook until softened, 3 to 4 minutes, stirring frequently. Add the beans, broth, cumin, chili powder, paprika, salt, and lime juice, and stir to combine. Cook until the beans are heated through and the liquid cooks down, 10 to 12 minutes. Smash the beans, using a potato masher, then stir in the lime zest.

For the shrimp, heat a large skillet over medium-high heat, and add the olive oil. Add the shrimp to the hot oil. Add the garlic powder, chili powder, cayenne pepper, black pepper, and salt to the pan, and stir to evenly cover the shrimp with the seasoning. Cook the shrimp, stirring frequently, for 3 to 5 minutes, until the shrimp is golden on the outside and no longer transparent on the inside.

To assemble the bowls, start with the rice as a base, followed by a dollop of the beans, fajita veggies, shrimp, cilantro, and the lime.

SWEET POTATO *and* BLACK BEAN BUDDHA BOWL

Can you imagine what happens when you combine sweet potatoes, chickpeas, and black beans in a Buddha bowl? Magic. Wonderful, mesmerizing, tasty magic.

The Sweet Potato and Black Bean Buddha Bowl is the ultimate lunch bowl. It has everything you can wish for in a lunch bowl—highly nutritious ingredients and a wonderful taste. Think sweet potatoes roasted with black beans and other veggies, quinoa, and chickpeas mixed with the perfect homemade tahini sauce.

FOR THE QUINOA
1 cup (180 g) multicolor quinoa
½ tsp sea salt
2 cups (480 ml) water

FOR THE SWEET POTATOES
2 large sweet potatoes, diced
2 tbsp (30 ml) olive oil
1 tsp sea salt
½ tsp garlic powder
1 tsp ground cumin
½ tsp chili powder
½ tsp paprika
¼ tsp ground black pepper
2 red bell peppers, sliced
1 (15-oz [425-g]) can black beans with no salt added, drained, rinsed, and patted dry

FOR THE CHICKPEAS
1 tbsp (15 ml) olive oil
1 (15-oz [425-g]) can chickpeas with no salt added, drained, rinsed, and patted dry
1 tsp ground cumin
½ tsp garlic powder
¼ tsp sea salt
¼ tsp ground black pepper

Preheat the oven to 425°F (220°C).

Rinse the quinoa in a fine-mesh sieve to remove any debris and dirt. In a deep saucepan, cook the quinoa over medium-high heat for 6 to 8 minutes tossing frequently, to toast the quinoa. It's done when the quinoa is no longer wet and begins to pop and turn golden brown. Add the salt and water and stir. Over medium-high heat, bring the water to a boil, then reduce the heat to a simmer, and cover the pan. Cook for 15 to 20 minutes, or until the water is absorbed and the quinoa doubles in size. Remove the pan from the heat, and fluff the quinoa with a fork. Set it aside.

For the potatoes, line a rimmed baking sheet with parchment paper. On the pan, toss the sweet potatoes, olive oil, salt, garlic powder, cumin, chili powder, paprika, and pepper until the potatoes are coated. Roast the potatoes for 15 minutes. Then, add the bell peppers, and toss to mix them with the potatoes.

Roast the potato mixture for another 15 to 20 minutes, or until the peppers are crisp-tender and the potatoes are tender. Remove the baking sheet from the oven, and toss the potato and pepper mixture with the black beans. Set aside.

For the chickpeas, heat the olive oil over medium-high heat in a large skillet. Add the chickpeas, cumin, garlic powder, salt, and pepper, and stir to combine. Cook, stirring frequently, until the chickpeas are crispy and golden brown, 10 to 12 minutes. Remove the pan from the heat, and set it aside.

(CONTINUED)

SWEET POTATO *and* BLACK BEAN BUDDHA BOWL (CONTINUED)

(CONTINUED)

FOR THE TAHINI SAUCE
¼ cup (57 g) tahini
1 tbsp (15 ml) freshly squeezed lemon juice
¼ tsp sea salt
¼ tsp garlic powder
⅛ tsp ground cumin
2–4 tbsp (30–60 ml) water, divided

FOR SERVING
Lime wedges
Cilantro

Meanwhile, for the sauce, combine the tahini, lemon juice, salt, garlic powder, and cumin in a small bowl, and whisk together until completely combined. If the sauce is too thick, whisk in the water, 2 tablespoons (30 ml) at a time, until you achieve a pourable, but not watery, consistency.

For serving, start with a base of quinoa in the bowl, and top with the sweet potato mixture, then the chickpeas. Drizzle the bowl with the tahini sauce, add the limes and cilantro, and serve.

Shockingly Healthy
APPETIZERS YOU CAN ENJOY AS A LUNCH

Appetizers are the life of a party, BBQ, or any gathering. There's something about bite-size food that makes it taste better and seem more fun. It might be the fact that cute food makes you appreciate the taste more, or the fact that sharing food with others makes the whole experience better.

All I know is that, when I turn appetizers into meals, I am a happy camper. Because they're naturally portioned out for smaller servings as appetizers, they are great for portion control, which is always a plus for anyone who wants to make food ahead of time, but not take time to divide the food into appropriate portions. Bonus: this makes them easy to pack for lunch, too!

The appetizers in this chapter are well rounded in that they contain balanced servings of veggies and/or complex carbs, good fats, and starches. That means they'll provide you with great sources of protein, fiber, and good fat in every serving.

This chapter has the guidance and inspiration you need to find the best and healthiest ways to turn appetizers into filling, delicious lunches. All the tasty appetizers I chose for this chapter are shockingly clean, although it will be hard to believe, because they taste so good. They're quick and easy to make, and so much fun to eat. Finger food? Count me in!

BUFFALO CAULIFLOWER "WINGS" *with* ZESTY RANCH DIPPING SAUCE

Buffalo chicken wings—the fried and dipped wings—are what everybody wants when watching a football game. Even without all-purpose flour, butter, and the high-sugar dipping sauce, these cauliflower wings are ah-mazing.

We get sneaky replacing the chicken with the cauliflower for added fiber and nutrients. The coating of almond flour and chickpea flour is high in fiber and protein, making these "wings" a great choice for lunch. Coated in a clean sauce and served with a clean ranch dip, these are better than any restaurant wings I've ever had on game day!

FOR THE CAULIFLOWER WINGS

1 cup (85 g) chickpea flour

1 cup (240 ml) unsweetened almond milk

1 tsp garlic powder

1 tsp paprika

½ tsp sea salt

½ tsp ground black pepper

2 cups (240 g) almond flour

½ tsp sea salt

1 large head cauliflower, broken into florets

FOR THE BUFFALO SAUCE

½ cup (120 ml) hot sauce (I like Frank's RedHot Original)

2 tbsp (30 g) coconut oil, melted

2 tbsp (30 ml) pure maple syrup

1 tbsp (15 ml) apple cider vinegar

1 tsp garlic powder

½ tsp sea salt

FOR THE SPICY RANCH DIP

1 cup (240 g) plain full-fat Greek yogurt

¼ cup (60 ml) unsweetened almond milk

1 tbsp (15 ml) apple cider vinegar

1 tbsp (3 g) chopped fresh Italian parsley, plus more for garnish

½ tsp onion powder

½ tsp coconut sugar

¼ tsp dried dill

¼ tsp sea salt

¼ tsp ground black pepper

For the cauliflower wings, preheat the oven to 450°F (230°C), and line a baking sheet with parchment paper.

In a mixing bowl, combine the chickpea flour, almond milk, garlic powder, paprika, salt, and pepper to make the batter.

In a separate bowl, combine the almond flour and salt.

Toss the cauliflower florets in the chickpea batter one at a time, shaking off any excess batter, then dip the floret in the almond flour mixture, and place it on the prepared baking sheet. Repeat until all of the florets are coated.

Bake the florets for 20 to 22 minutes.

Make the sauce while the florets are baking. In a large bowl, combine the hot sauce, coconut oil, maple syrup, vinegar, garlic powder, and salt. Set aside the sauce.

Remove the cauliflower from the oven, and toss it into the sauce to coat it. Return the cauliflower to the baking sheet, and bake it for another 5 minutes to allow the sauce to soak in.

To make the ranch dip, combine the yogurt, milk, vinegar, parsley, onion powder, coconut sugar, dill, salt, and pepper in a mixing bowl, and whisk until smooth. Refrigerate the dip until it's needed.

Remove the cauliflower from the oven, and serve immediately with the ranch dip and extra parsley.

COCONUT SHRIMP *with* SPICY MANGO DIPPING SAUCE

Tell me you don't like coconut shrimp—I dare you! They're just impossible not to enjoy, if you ask me. The combination of the savory coating with the sweet, crunchy coconut is so yummy. I love to pair it with a spicy mango dipping sauce to contrast the sweet with spicy. Plus, any chance I get, I'll add mangoes because they're so tasty and good for you.

This appetizer-turned-lunch has amazing tropical flavors and is so incredibly delicious that it's definitely one to add to your list of regular recipes. Kiddos will love it, too!

FOR THE COCONUT SHRIMP
1 egg
2 egg whites
½ cup (40 g) unsweetened shredded coconut
1 tsp paprika
1 tsp onion powder
1 tsp garlic powder
½ tsp sea salt
20 large, raw deveined shrimp
3 tbsp (16 g) chickpea flour

FOR THE SPICY MANGO DIPPING SAUCE
1¼ cups (300 g) plain full-fat Greek yogurt
½ cup (80 g) mango chunks
¼ cup (4 g) roughly chopped fresh cilantro
1 tbsp (15 ml) freshly squeezed lime juice
½ jalapeño pepper, seeded
¼ tsp sea salt

For the shrimp, preheat the oven to 400°F (200°C), and line a rimmed baking sheet with parchment paper.

Whisk together the egg and the egg whites in a medium bowl.

In a separate large bowl, combine the coconut, paprika, onion powder, garlic powder, and salt.

Pat the shrimp dry, and then toss it in a medium bowl or resealable plastic bag with the chickpea flour. Dip 1 shrimp at a time into the egg mixture, then into the coconut mixture, then place the shrimp on the prepared baking pan, being careful not to crowd them. Once all of the shrimp are coated, bake them for 15 to 20 minutes, or until they are golden brown and crunchy.

Make the sauce while the shrimp is in the oven. Combine the yogurt, mango, cilantro, lime juice, jalapeño, and salt in a high-speed blender, and blend until smooth.

Note: Make sure to purchase unsweetened shredded coconut to avoid unnecessary added sugars.

HUMMUS PLATE *with* FLATBREAD *and* GREEK SALAD

Hummus is always appreciated by those who embrace clean eating, because it feels like a decadent dip when you eat it: it's fun, flavorful, and full of protein. It's versatile and, despite the fact that it's technically an appetizer, it's not at all hard to make it into a delicious lunch. Pair it with a salad and flatbread, and your lunch is ready. And it will include all the nutrients you need to continue your day. Win!

This lunch plate includes the traditional hummus made with chickpeas and tahini, a Greek salad made with romaine lettuce, red onion, Kalamata olives, grape tomatoes, cucumber, feta cheese, and a simple salad dressing, plus whole-grain flatbread. Such a great combo of flavors!

FOR THE HUMMUS

1 (15-oz [425-g]) can chickpeas with no salt added, drained and rinsed
Juice of 1 large lemon
¼ cup (57 g) tahini
1 clove garlic
2 tbsp (30 ml) olive oil
½ tsp ground cumin
¾ tsp sea salt
2–3 tbsp (30–45 ml) water, divided

FOR THE GREEK DRESSING

¼ cup (60 ml) olive oil
¼ cup (60 ml) red wine vinegar
1 tbsp (15 ml) freshly squeezed lemon juice
1 clove garlic, minced
1 tsp Dijon mustard
1 tsp dried oregano
1 tsp raw honey
½ tsp sea salt
¼ tsp ground black pepper

FOR THE SIMPLE GREEK SALAD

1 head romaine lettuce, chopped
1 red onion, thinly sliced
½ cup (90 g) Kalamata olives
½ cup (80 g) grape tomatoes, halved
1 cucumber, sliced
1 cup (150 g) crumbled feta cheese

FOR SERVING

2 pieces whole-grain flatbread or pita bread, sliced into thin strips
1 tsp hemp seed hearts

To make the hummus, in the bowl of a food processor, add the chickpeas, lemon juice, tahini, garlic, olive oil, cumin, and salt, and process until smooth. Depending on the texture you're looking for, you'll probably need to add water to the mixture to make it very smooth. I usually need to add 2 to 3 tablespoons (30 to 45 ml), but I add them 1 tablespoon (15 ml) at a time to be safe. Refrigerate the hummus while you continue with the recipe.

To make the Greek dressing, in a small mixing bowl, whisk together the olive oil, vinegar, lemon juice, garlic, mustard, oregano, honey, salt, and pepper.

For the salad, combine the lettuce, onion, olives, tomatoes, cucumber, and feta in a large salad bowl. Drizzle with the salad dressing, and then toss to coat.

To serve, arrange half of the Greek salad on one side of a bowl. In the empty portion of the bowl, add about ⅓ cup (80 g) of the hummus, and then lay the flatbread next to the hummus, for dipping. Lightly sprinkle half of the hemp seed hearts over the entire bowl. Repeat with the remaining ingredients and another bowl and serve.

Refrigerate the remaining hummus in an airtight container for up to 5 days.

Note: Add the dressing just before serving if you are preparing this salad ahead.

PORK CARNITAS MINI TOSTADAS *with* SPICY BLACK BEANS

Tender, juicy, and crispy Mexican pork carnitas is another appetizer that I believe should be on our table more often . . . with a few adjustments, of course. And I can happily say the same thing about black beans mini tostadas.

Traditionally, pork carnitas are made with Mexican Coca-Cola, but if you want your lunch to be free of refined sugar, you'll skip the coke and cook the pork, seasoned with spices, in a little bit of olive oil. The meat will still be tender and juicy, just, you know, healthier. When the pork is done, make the Spicy Black Beans, then assemble everything onto the crispy tortillas, and top with all the goodness. Satisfying, and finger-licking good.

FOR THE CARNITAS
1½ tsp (3 g) ground cumin
½ tsp sea salt
½ tsp chili powder
½ tsp coconut sugar
¼ tsp dried oregano
⅛ tsp garlic powder
⅛ tsp cayenne pepper
½ lb (230 g) pork tenderloin, cut into 1" (2.5-cm) chunks
1 tbsp (15 ml) olive oil
¼ cup (60 ml) low-sodium chicken broth
2 tbsp (30 ml) freshly squeezed orange juice

FOR THE SPICY BLACK BEANS
1 tbsp (15 ml) olive oil
1 jalapeño pepper, seeded and minced
1 clove garlic, minced
1 (15-oz [425-g]) can black beans with no salt added, drained and rinsed
¼ cup (60 ml) vegetable broth
1 tbsp (15 ml) freshly squeezed lime juice
½ tsp ground cumin
½ tsp chili powder
½ tsp paprika
½ tsp sea salt
⅛ tsp cayenne pepper

FOR THE YOGURT-LIME SAUCE
¼ cup (60 g) plain full-fat Greek yogurt
3 tbsp (45 ml) freshly squeezed lime juice
2–3 tbsp (30–45 ml) unsweetened almond milk, divided

For the carnitas, in a medium bowl, mix well the cumin, salt, chili powder, coconut sugar, oregano, garlic powder, and cayenne pepper. Add the pork, and toss it with the seasoning mix to coat.

In a large skillet, heat the olive oil over medium-high heat. Add the pork in a single layer in the skillet. Cook for 6 to 8 minutes, or until the meat is cooked through, and golden brown on all sides. Add the chicken broth and orange juice, cover, and reduce the heat to medium. Cook the pork for 10 minutes, or until it's tender. Remove the pork from the heat, and pull it apart using two forks to make shredded carnitas.

Meanwhile, prepare the black beans. Heat the olive oil over medium-high heat in a skillet, then add the jalapeño and garlic, and cook until softened, 3 to 4 minutes, stirring frequently. Add the beans, broth, lime juice, cumin, chili powder, paprika, salt, and cayenne, and stir to combine. Cook until the beans are heated through and the liquid cooks down, 4 to 6 minutes. Then, mash the beans using a potato masher until they are mostly smooth, but still a little chunky.

For the yogurt-lime sauce, in a small bowl, combine the yogurt, lime juice, and 2 tablespoons (30 ml) of the almond milk, and whisk together. The texture should be thin enough to drizzle; if it's not, add more of the remaining milk until it is.

Set aside.

(CONTINUED)

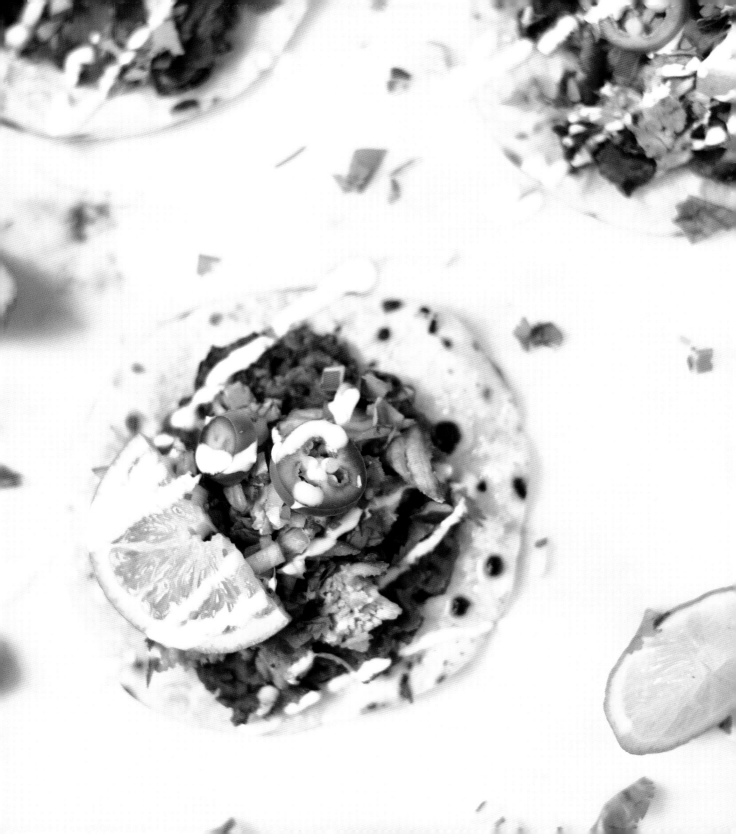

PORK CARNITAS MINI TOSTADAS *with* SPICY BLACK BEANS (CONTINUED)

FOR THE TOSTADAS

1 tbsp (15 ml) olive oil, divided

6 small cassava flour tortillas

FOR SERVING

¼ cup (4 g) chopped fresh cilantro

Lime wedges

2 tbsp (20 g) diced red onion

For the tostadas, heat a skillet or griddle over high heat. Add 1 teaspoon of the olive oil to the pan, then lay 2 to 3 of the tortillas flat in the pan, taking care not to crowd them. Cook on both sides, until they are golden brown and beginning to become crisp and slightly burnt, 1 to 2 minutes per side. Keep the tortillas warm by stacking and wrapping them in a clean dish towel or paper towels. Repeat the cooking process with the remaining tortillas, adding more of the olive oil, 1 teaspoon at a time, as needed.

To serve, spread the beans evenly onto the tortillas. Spoon the pork mixture over the beans. Top with the cilantro, lime, onion, and a drizzle of the yogurt-lime sauce.

STEAK *and* BLUE CHEESE SLIDERS

I've got to say, I'm not usually the biggest fan of blue cheese. *But* put these sliders in front of me and I just can't help myself. They're made with whole-grain slider buns, deliciously seasoned New York strip steak, and the most amazing blue cheese dressing I've ever tasted. They're so good, you'll forget they're homemade and actually good for you!

FOR THE BLUE CHEESE DRESSING

2 tbsp (30 g) plain full-fat Greek yogurt

½ tsp freshly squeezed lemon juice

¼ tsp apple cider vinegar

1–2 tbsp (15–30 ml) unsweetened almond milk, divided

1 tbsp (10 g) crumbled blue cheese

½ tsp sea salt

¼ tsp ground black pepper

FOR THE STEAK

1 (12-oz [340-g]) grass-fed New York strip steaks

1 tsp sea salt

½ tsp ground black pepper

¼ tsp garlic powder

1 tbsp (15 ml) olive oil

FOR THE SLIDERS

4 whole-grain slider buns

4 leaves butter lettuce

Red onion, thinly sliced into rings

For the blue cheese dressing, place the yogurt, lemon juice, vinegar, almond milk, blue cheese, salt, and pepper in a small bowl. Mix until well combined. Refrigerate the dressing while you prepare the sliders.

For the steak, season the meat by sprinkling it evenly with the salt, pepper, and garlic powder. Heat a large skillet over high heat. Add the oil to the pan and swirl to coat. Add the steak to the pan, and cook it for 3 minutes on each side, or until browned. Reduce the heat to medium-low, and cook for 1½ minutes longer.

Remove the steak from the pan, and let it rest for 5 minutes. Slice the steak diagonally across the grain into very thin slices.

While the steak is resting, toast the buns. Preheat the broiler to high, and line a baking sheet with aluminum foil. Arrange the buns, cut side up, on the baking sheet, and broil them for 1 to 2 minutes, or until they are golden.

Spread the blue cheese dressing on the top and bottom sides of each bun. Arrange the lettuce, then the sliced steak, and the red onion on the bottom of the buns. Top with the other side of the bun and serve.

See image on page 156.

SHRIMP SUMMER ROLLS *with* SPICY PEANUT DIPPING SAUCE

Summer rolls, all wrapped up and ready to enjoy, are the perfect bite-size appetizer, treat, and snack. There are so many flavor combinations and they're so fresh and yummy. One of my favorite combinations is seasoned shrimp with fresh veggies, paired with a spicy peanut dipping sauce. Summer rolls are fun to eat, filling, and full of fresh flavors—making them a great lunch. Plus they look super cool and are crazy quick to make.

FOR THE SPICY PEANUT DIPPING SAUCE

2 tbsp (30 g) natural peanut butter

2 tsp (10 ml) sesame oil

1 tbsp (15 ml) freshly squeezed lime juice, plus more for garnish

1 tbsp (15 ml) low-sodium soy sauce

2 tsp (10 ml) rice vinegar

¼ tsp ground ginger

¼ tsp crushed red pepper flakes

1–2 tbsp (15–30 ml) warm water, divided, optional

FOR THE SUMMER ROLLS

12 round rice paper wrappers

1 head (12 leaves) butter or Bibb lettuce

⅛ small red cabbage, thinly sliced

2 carrots, cut into matchsticks

1 medium cucumber, cut into matchsticks

12–16 mint leaves

1 cup (20 g) microgreens or bean sprouts

1 lb (455 g) large, deveined cooked shrimp, sliced in half lengthwise

For the dipping sauce, in a small saucepan, heat the peanut butter, sesame oil, lime juice, soy sauce, rice vinegar, ginger, and crushed red pepper flakes over medium-high heat. Stir the sauce until it's smooth. If you desire a thinner consistency for dipping, add the water, 1 tablespoon (15 ml) at a time, until you reach your preferred thickness. Remove the sauce from the heat while you prepare the summer rolls.

Arrange the wrappers, lettuce, cabbage, carrots, cucumber, mint, microgreens, and shrimp in an assembly line.

One rice paper at a time, dip the wrapper in hot water for 10 to 15 seconds. Lay the wrapper flat on a cutting board. Starting at the bottom third of wrapper, add the lettuce, cabbage, carrots, cucumber, mint, and microgreens, then top with the shrimp.

Fold the bottom of the wrapper up over the ingredients. Fold in the sides, then continue rolling up. Place seam side down on a plate. Repeat with the remaining ingredients. Serve the summer rolls with the dipping sauce and a lime wedge.

YOU-WON'T-BELIEVE-THESE-ARE-CLEAN LOADED POTATO SKINS

Truly, you won't believe that these are clean loaded potato skins. They are hearty, satisfying, cheesy, and tasty. Basically, they are just like the loaded potato skins you're used to, with just a few very easy tweaks. How amazing! To make these, you'll need cheddar cheese, sugar- and nitrate-free bacon, green onion, and plain full-fat Greek yogurt. I bet you're already picturing yourself enjoying these potato skins for lunch!

FOR THE SKINS

4 medium russet potatoes

1–2 tbsp (15–30 ml) olive oil, divided

1½ tsp (10 g) sea salt, divided

6 slices sugar-free, nitrate-free bacon (I like Pederson's Uncured No Sugar Added Hickory Smoked)

¼ tsp ground black pepper

⅛ tsp garlic powder

¾ cup (85 g) shredded cheddar cheese

FOR SERVING

¼ cup (60 g) plain full-fat Greek yogurt

1 tbsp (15 ml) hot sauce (I like Frank's RedHot Original)

1–2 tbsp (15–30 ml) unsweetened almond milk, divided

4 green onions, sliced

For the skins, preheat your oven to 400°F (200°C).

Scrub the potatoes and dry them well, then coat each one with a thin layer of the olive oil, about 1 tablespoon (15 ml), using your hands. Sprinkle ¾ teaspoon of the salt around the potatoes, and wrap them in aluminum foil. Place them on a rimmed baking sheet, and bake them for 60 to 70 minutes, until they are tender when gently squeezed with an oven mitt or clean kitchen towel. Alternatively, you can microwave the potatoes without aluminum foil on a microwave-safe plate for 8 to 12 minutes, or until tender. Allow the potatoes to cool until you can handle them.

While the potatoes are in the oven, heat a skillet over medium heat, and add the bacon. Cook, stirring occasionally, for even browning. Once crisp, in 8 to 10 minutes, remove the slices with a slotted spoon to drain on paper towels. Crumble the bacon, then set it aside.

Line a rimmed baking sheet with parchment paper.

Remove the foil, and slice each potato in half, lengthwise. Using a spoon, scoop out most of the flesh of the potato. You can save the flesh for homemade mashed potatoes, but it will not be used in this recipe. Leave some potato lining the shell of the potato skin.

Set the potato skins onto the baking sheet. Drizzle with the remaining 1 tablespoon (15 ml) of the olive oil and rub it around the inside of the skins. Season the skins with the remaining ¾ teaspoon of salt, and the pepper and garlic powder. Bake the skins for 5 minutes, or until they are golden brown and are beginning to get crisp. Then flip them face down, and bake for another 5 minutes, or until both sides are crisp. Remove the skins from the oven, and preheat the broiler to high.

Fill each potato skin with one-eighth of the cheddar cheese and bacon crumbles, and then place the pan under the broiler for 1 to 2 minutes to heat through and to melt the cheese.

For serving, mix together the yogurt and hot sauce in a small mixing bowl. Add 1 tablespoon (15 ml) of the almond milk and mix it in. Add as much of the remaining almond milk as needed to make the sauce runny enough to drizzle. Top the skins with the green onions and drizzle with the sauce.

Delicious, Nutritious, PILED-HIGH SANDWICHES

Sandwiches are versatile and easy to make. They are perfect for lunch boxes, but they can be good for breakfast, dinner, and for snacks as well. Few meal choices are quicker and easier and nothing beats their simplicity. The problem is—one simple sandwich can pack hundreds of calories and can be full of unhealthy, overly fatty ingredients.

Additionally, most sandwiches are made with white bread, mayo, high-sodium deli meats or cold cuts, and other high-calorie, high-fat, or high-carb toppings. The calories, fats, and carbs add up fast. While all you want to do is make a quick and delicious lunch, you end up making a sandwich that's not at all good for your health and ruins your progress toward eating clean.

Here's the thing though: You can turn these lunch staples into clean and incredibly satisfying meals. And you don't have to struggle to do it. Load them with fresh veggies or fruits, use a light spread instead of mayo or butter, fill them with lean protein, and use the right bread. These changes will turn any sandwich into a nourishing meal without taking away the simplicity or the amazing taste.

CHICKPEA MEATBALLS SUB

Submarine sandwiches—also known as *heros*, *grinders*, *hoagies*, and *poor boys*—are like the holy grail of sandwiches. The large oblong rolls crowded with meats, cheeses, veggies, sauce, and other toppings and condiments are the epitome of delicious sandwiches. One of the most popular sub sandwiches has to be the one with meatballs and marinara. It's hard to resist. It's so hearty and so good.

This Chickpea Meatballs Sub is not only a healthier and better-for-you option, but also vegan. This delish sub is made with chickpea meatballs and a homemade marinara sauce and assembled on a whole-grain sub roll. Vegan or not, you'll find the Chickpea Meatballs Sub filling, flavorful, and delicious.

FOR THE CHICKPEA MEATBALLS
1½ tbsp (10 g) ground flaxseed
½–¾ cup (120–180 ml) water, divided
1 (15-oz [425-g]) can chickpeas with no salt added, drained and rinsed
½–⅔ cup (60–80 g) almond flour, divided
2 tsp (6 g) garlic powder
2 tsp (5 g) onion powder
1 tbsp (3 g) chopped fresh Italian parsley
½ tsp sea salt
1 tsp dried basil
¼ tsp ground black pepper

FOR THE MARINARA SAUCE
½ cup (120 g) tomato paste
½ cup (120 ml) vegetable broth
1 tsp dried thyme
1 tsp dried basil
1 tsp dried oregano
¼ tsp garlic powder
½ tsp sea salt
1 tsp pure maple syrup

FOR THE SUBS
4 whole-grain sub rolls, sliced in half
6 leaves fresh basil, thinly sliced

For the chickpea meatballs, preheat the oven to 400°F (200°C), and line a rimmed baking sheet with parchment paper.

Mix the ground flaxseed with ½ cup (120 ml) of the water in a small bowl, then set it aside for 5 minutes to make flax egg.

In a food processor, place the flaxseed mixture, chickpeas, ½ cup (60 g) of the almond flour, garlic powder, onion powder, parsley, salt, basil, and pepper. Process until the mixture is smooth and is a consistency that is easy to roll without sticking to your hands or cracking. Add more of the remaining ¼ cup (60 ml) of water, a little at a time, if the mixture is too dry. If the mixture is too sticky, add more of the remaining 2 tablespoons (20 g) of almond flour a little at a time.

Shape the mixture into 2-inch (5-cm) balls using your hands, and then place the balls on the prepared baking sheet. Bake for 16 to 18 minutes, or until the meatballs start to brown.

Prepare the marinara while the meatballs are baking. In a medium saucepan, place the tomato paste, vegetable broth, thyme, basil, oregano, garlic powder, salt, and maple syrup. Cook over medium-high heat until the sauce is heated through, 4 to 6 minutes.

For the subs, spread the marinara sauce on the bottom of each bun. Add 3 to 4 of the meatballs, depending on the size of your roll, and then top the meatballs with more marinara sauce and the basil.

Note: Chickpea meatballs are great in vegan form, but if you are not vegan, you can replace the flaxseed and water with one egg. You can also top the subs with grated fresh mozzarella and Parmesan, as sub shops do with traditional meatball subs.

FRESH TUNA MELT QUESADILLA

Tuna sandwiches are so simple, so easy, and they require only a few ingredients—usually canned tuna, mayo, and, sometimes, celery or onion. You've got to love a classic. Fortunately, tuna sandwiches can easily be made clean by replacing the mayo with Greek yogurt. However, that's not what I want to talk to you about.

While I agree that nothing beats a classic, I have a tasty proposition for you. What do you think about transforming the tuna sandwich into a delicious quesadilla? This Fresh Tuna Melt Quesadilla combines two delicious lunches. You get the best of both worlds if you make this quesadilla: the crunchy tortilla and cheesy goodness, and the amazing taste of the classic tuna sandwich.

FOR THE TUNA SALAD
1 tbsp (15 ml) olive oil
1 lb (455 g) fresh tuna steaks
¼ tsp sea salt
¼ tsp ground black pepper
¼ cup (40 g) finely diced red onion
1 clove garlic, minced
2 ribs celery, finely diced
½ whole dill pickle, finely diced
1 tbsp (15 ml) dill pickle juice
½ tsp dried oregano
¼ tsp lemon zest
⅓ cup (80 g) plain full-fat Greek yogurt

FOR THE QUESADILLAS
3–4 tsp (15–20 ml) olive oil, divided
8 cassava flour or whole wheat flour tortillas
1 cup (115 g) shredded Monterey Jack cheese

FOR SERVING
½ avocado, thinly sliced
1 large tomato, thinly sliced

For the tuna salad, heat the oil in a skillet over medium-high heat. Season both sides of the tuna steaks with the salt and pepper. When the oil is hot, add the tuna steaks, and cook until they are lightly browned on each side and cooked through, 4 to 5 minutes per side. Chop the tuna into bite-size pieces, then set it aside to cool.

In a mixing bowl, combine the onion, garlic, celery, pickle, pickle juice, oregano, and lemon zest. Add the chopped tuna and yogurt to the bowl, and fold together.

For the quesadillas, heat 1 teaspoon of the olive oil in a large skillet over medium-high heat. Lay 1 tortilla flat on the skillet. Evenly spread about ¾ cup (255 g) of the tuna mixture on the tortilla. Sprinkle approximately 2 to 3 tablespoons (14 to 21 g) of the cheese over the tuna, top it with another tortilla, and press it down to seal.

Cook each quesadilla until it's golden brown and the cheese is melted, 2 to 4 minutes per side. Repeat with the remaining ingredients. To keep the cooked quesadillas warm, cover them with a clean kitchen towel.

For serving, cut the quesadillas into wedges, and top with the avocado and tomato.

GREEN GODDESS GRILLED CHEESE

The gooey grilled cheese sandwich had to be here because, in my opinion, this sandwich is a timeless classic that makes so many people happy. With three types of cheese and grilled to get the amazing grilled cheese texture, this sandwich brings the grilled cheese to a whole new level of healthiness and deliciousness! Wondering why it's called a Green Goddess Grilled Cheese? Because, instead of a butter spread, the sandwich is made with Green Goddess Pesto, filled with ingredients to up the nutrition. To grill the sandwich, you'll need just a tiny bit of olive oil—no need for loads of butter to get that crispy, golden crust.

FOR THE GREEN GODDESS PESTO

1 clove garlic

1 small shallot, roughly chopped

1 tsp freshly squeezed lemon juice

1 handful fresh Italian parsley, chopped

1 handful kale, chopped

¼ cup (20 g) grated Parmesan cheese

1 large green onion, chopped

¼ tsp sea salt

⅛ tsp ground black pepper

¼ cup (60 ml) olive oil

FOR THE GRILLED CHEESE

4 slices whole-grain bread

4 (1½-oz [40-g]) slices Monterey Jack cheese, divided

½ avocado, sliced

2 tbsp (35 g) crumbled goat cheese

1 handful fresh baby spinach

2 tsp (10 ml) olive oil, divided

To make the pesto, process the garlic, shallot, lemon juice, parsley, kale, Parmesan, green onion, salt, and pepper in a food processor until the mixture is chopped. Slowly drizzle in the olive oil until the texture resembles the consistency of a pesto, scraping down the sides of the bowl, as needed.

Spread about 1 tablespoon (16 g) of the pesto onto each slice of bread. On 2 slices of the bread, layer one slice of the cheese, half of the avocado, goat cheese, and spinach, and another slice of cheese. Top with the remaining bread. Press the slices of bread together gently.

Heat 1 teaspoon of the olive oil in a skillet over medium-low heat. Add one sandwich to the oil, and cook it until the bread is golden brown. Press down on the sandwich lightly, then flip it over, and cook until the second side is golden brown. Remove the sandwich from the pan and set it aside while you cook the second sandwich. Use the remaining teaspoon of olive oil, if needed, to grease the pan.

Slice in half, and serve immediately.

MILE-HIGH VEGGIE SANDWICH

The easiest way to make a clean sandwich is to take two slices of whole-grain bread, use a creamy avocado spread, then add as many veggie toppings as possible. Simple, but surprisingly delicious if you get out of your comfort zone a little bit and you combine veggies with different flavors and textures with seeds and greens.

If a veggie sandwich sounds like something you would love, the Mile-High Veggie Sandwich is the perfect recipe for you. Made with avocado, sesame seeds, sunflower seeds, butter lettuce, carrot, red cabbage, tomato, and red onion, the Mile-High Veggie Sandwich is high in fiber, vitamins, and minerals, but low in carbs and calories.

2 slices whole-grain bread

½ small avocado

⅛ tsp sea salt

⅛ tsp ground black pepper

⅛ tsp black sesame seeds

1½ tsp (5 g) raw sunflower seeds

4 leaves butter lettuce

½ small cucumber, thinly sliced

1 small carrot, julienned

⅛ head red cabbage, thinly sliced

1 medium tomato, sliced

¼ small red onion, thinly sliced

Toast the bread until crisp, so it does not get soggy. Set it aside.

In a small bowl, mash the avocado until it is mostly smooth. Mix in the salt, pepper, and sesame seeds.

Spread half of the mashed avocado over one side of each slice of toast. Sprinkle one slice with the sunflower seeds.

Over the sunflower seeds, layer half the lettuce so it evenly fits the size of bread, then add the cucumber, carrot, cabbage, tomato, and onion. Then add the remaining lettuce, and top it with the other slice of toast.

Wrap the sandwich tightly in parchment paper to help hold it together. Slice the sandwich in half and serve.

NOT-YOUR-MOM'S CHICKEN SALAD SANDWICH

Do you remember your mom's chicken salad? It had tender chicken, celery, mayo, and maybe some types of nuts and apple slices for added texture. It was so simple, yet everybody loved it. There was nothing wrong with the taste, but high calories and fat left a lot missing when it came to nutrition.

Enter the Not-Your-Mom's Chicken Salad Sandwich, made with avocado instead of mayo, chicken breast, crisp apple, red onion, and dried cranberries. It's nothing like the classic chicken salad; it's better and way more delicious, but just as easy to make.

FOR THE AVOCADO CHICKEN SALAD

1 avocado, diced

1 cup (140 g) cooked shredded chicken breast

½ Granny Smith apple, cored and finely diced

¼ cup (40 g) finely diced red onion

½ tbsp (4 g) dried cranberries with no sugar added

1 tsp freshly squeezed lemon juice

¼ tsp sea salt

¼ tsp ground black pepper

⅛ tsp garlic powder

FOR THE SANDWICHES

4 slices whole-grain bread or whole wheat pita bread

6 leaves butter lettuce

1 large tomato, sliced

¼ cup (5 g) microgreens

For the chicken salad, mash the avocado in a medium mixing bowl, until it is mostly pureed. Add the chicken, apple, onion, cranberries, lemon juice, salt, pepper, and garlic powder, and mix together well.

For the sandwiches, on each of 2 slices of bread, layer half of the lettuce, tomato, and microgreens. Top the greens with half of the chicken salad and remaining slices of bread. Serve immediately.

TANGY LENTIL SLOPPY JOES

A Sloppy Joe—the classic sandwich made with ground beef and spicy tomato sauce, usually including Worcestershire sauce, mustard, and seasonings—is served in a burger bun. It is not just a classic but *the classic,* that every American knows by heart. I'm going to teach you how to make it lighter and healthier, because I'm all about that kind of stuff and we all need some more Sloppy Joes in our lives, am I right?

These Tangy Lentil Sloppy Joes are a vegan and lightened-up version of the American classic. To add extra flair and texture, I top them with some quick, homemade pickled onions (which are super fun and yummy!). These amazing Sloppy Joes are not only great served over a toasted whole-grain burger bun, they are just as delicious on a baked potato.

FOR THE QUICK PICKLED ONIONS

1 medium red onion, very thinly sliced
½ cup (120 ml) water
¼ cup (60 ml) distilled white vinegar
¼ cup (60 ml) apple cider vinegar
1½ tbsp (23 ml) pure maple syrup
1½ tsp (4 g) sea salt

FOR THE TANGY LENTILS

1 cup (192 g) green lentils
4 cups (960 ml) water
1 tbsp (15 ml) olive oil
1 medium yellow onion, finely diced
1 medium red bell pepper, finely diced
2 cloves garlic, minced
3 tbsp (23 g) chili powder
2 tsp (4 g) paprika
1 (15-oz [425-g]) can no-salt tomato sauce
2 tbsp (30 g) tomato paste
1 tbsp (6 g) dry mustard
2 tbsp (30 ml) pure maple syrup
1 tbsp (15 ml) apple cider vinegar
1 tsp sea salt

FOR SERVING

4 whole-grain wheat burger buns, toasted

To make the pickled onions, press the red onion into a 1-pint (480-ml) Mason jar or similar heat-safe container. Place the jar in the sink, as this will help to catch any splashes of hot vinegar later.

In a small saucepan, combine the water, white vinegar, cider vinegar, maple syrup, and salt. Bring the mixture to a gentle simmer over medium heat, then carefully pour the heated mixture into the jar over the onions.

Use a spoon to press the onions down into the vinegar and remove any air bubbles in the jar. Let the pickled onions cool to room temperature, 25 to 30 minutes, before serving.

For the lentils, in a deep saucepan or stockpot, bring the lentils and water to a boil over high heat. Reduce the heat to medium and simmer for 18 to 20 minutes, or until the lentils are tender. Drain the water, and set aside the lentils.

Heat a large skillet over medium-high heat, and add the olive oil. Once hot, add the onion, red bell pepper, and garlic. Cook for 4 to 6 minutes, or until the onion starts to sweat. Then, add the chili powder and paprika, and stir to coat. Add the tomato sauce, tomato paste, dry mustard, maple syrup, vinegar, and salt. Stir until well incorporated, then stir in the lentils.

Serve the Sloppy Joes, topped with the pickled onions, on the burger buns.

Note: Any remaining pickled onions can be stored in a covered jar in the refrigerator for up to 7 days. Besides on Sloppy Joes, we enjoy them on tacos and in salads.

EGGPLANT GYRO *with* TZATZIKI SAUCE

Gyro, the Greek sandwich, is traditionally made with lamb (or other meats, such as pork, beef, or chicken), tomatoes, onions, cucumbers, and tzatziki—a cucumber-yogurt sauce—all served on pita bread. This eggplant gyro is made with eggplant to up the nutritional value and fiber, plus to find a way to sneak in more veggies!

This tzatziki sauce is life. It's made with cashews, cucumber, almond milk, and a few spices and herbs, and is so fresh and flavorful. It's the perfect cool creaminess to complement the savory eggplant gyro. For toppings, I recommend the classics: tomato, red onion, cucumber, and parsley. As for bread, you've gotta go with the pita if you want an authentic gyro experience—but look for whole-grain pita or naan to keep the recipe as clean as possible.

FOR THE TZATZIKI SAUCE

½ cup (70 g) raw cashews

1 tbsp (15 g) tahini

1 clove garlic

½ large cucumber, diced

1 tbsp (10 g) hemp seeds

2–3 tbsp (30–45 ml) unsweetened almond milk, divided

2 tsp (2 g) chopped fresh dill

2 tsp (6 g) chopped fresh Italian parsley

2 tbsp (30 ml) freshly squeezed lemon juice

½ tsp sea salt

¼ tsp ground black pepper

FOR THE EGGPLANT

½ tsp sea salt

½ tsp ground black pepper

1½ tsp (2 g) dried oregano

2 medium eggplants, cut into ½" (12-mm) slices

1 tbsp (15 ml) olive oil

FOR THE GYROS

4 whole-wheat pitas or naan, warmed

½ large cucumber, thinly sliced

1 large tomato, sliced

½ medium red onion, thinly sliced

2 tbsp (6 g) chopped fresh Italian parsley, plus more for garnish, optional

For the tzatziki sauce, in a medium bowl, cover the cashews in boiling water, and let them sit for 1 hour, or up to overnight, to soften them.

Prepare the eggplant while the cashews soak. In a small mixing bowl, combine the salt, pepper, and oregano. Sprinkle this seasoning mixture on all sides of the eggplant to coat it evenly.

Heat the olive oil in a skillet over medium-high heat. Add the eggplant slices, in batches so as not to crowd them, and cook for 8 to 10 minutes, or until the eggplant is mostly tender. Set aside the eggplant.

To finish the tzatziki sauce, in a food processor, combine the drained soaked cashews, tahini, garlic, cucumber, hemp seeds, 2 tablespoons (30 ml) of the almond milk, dill, parsley, lemon juice, salt, and pepper, and process until smooth. The mixture should be thick, but pourable. If it needs to be thinner, add more of the remaining 1 tablespoon (15 ml) of milk, as needed.

To make the gyros, divide the eggplant among the pita breads and top it with the cucumber, tomato, onion, and parsley. Drizzle the gyros with the tzatziki sauce.

Wrap the gyros tightly in foil to help them hold together, and serve immediately. Garnish with parsley, if desired.

Note: Store any leftover tzatziki sauce in an airtight container in the fridge for up to 5 days. Use it as a multipurpose sauce.

ACKNOWLEDGMENTS

First and foremost, I'd like to thank my amazing husband and best friend, Dustin Baier. Dustin, thank you so much for your incredible support, not just with helping me bring this cookbook to life, but also for being my rock and helping me to achieve so much. I wouldn't be here without you, and I owe so much to you.

I'd also like to thank my sweet little nuggets, Jordan, Savannah, Hunter, and Carolina. Thank you for keeping me honest with making my healthy food taste good through your (at times reluctant) taste-testing assistance. Thank you also for dealing with cold food, so Mommy can take pictures, and for dealing with me trying to turn everything healthy.

Thank you to Page Street Publishing for providing me with an opportunity to push myself and to share my recipes and photos in a brand-new way. I am so grateful for the support and consider it such an awesome opportunity.

Finally, to all my readers and fans of A Sweet Pea Chef, thank you so much for your support. I couldn't have done this without you!

ABOUT *the* AUTHOR

Lacey Baier is the owner and editor of the food and health site, A Sweet Pea Chef. Lacey is known by her fans for providing easy-to-follow, clever, and clean-eating ways to enjoy the foods they love by using whole, real ingredients and simple steps. Her recipes and videos are enjoyed by millions of followers each month across her social channels and blog.

Lacey lives in Dallas, Texas, with her husband and business partner, Dustin, and their four children, Jordan, 9, Savannah, 7, Hunter, 5, and Carolina, 1. Making the decision to start eating healthier, paying attention to which types of foods she was choosing, learning what was in her foods, and changing the way she thought about food, dieting, and healthy living totally changed Lacey's life. She learned how to stop battling with her food, love who she is, and enjoy life in the process.

Along the way, she has lost 60-plus pounds twice, using clean eating and a sensible approach to making nutritious food taste delicious. She enjoys helping others become passionate about their food and clean-eating lifestyle and leave behind their battles with weight and food.

Lacey has been featured on various websites and podcasts, including *The Huffington Post*, BuzzFeed, Food Network, *Good Morning America*, Fox News, *Food Blogger Pro*, Tastemade, *Wellpreneur*, *Internet Business Mastery*, *Fitness Magazine*, and many more.

INDEX